The Extraordinary Mrs. R

Other books by William Turner Levy

William Barnes: The Man and the Poems

Affectionately, T. S. Eliot: The Story of a Friendship, 1947–1965 (with Victor Scherle)

The Films of Frank Capra (with Victor Scherle)

The Complete Films of Frank Capra (with Victor Scherle)

The Extraordinary Mrs. R

A Friend Remembers Eleanor Roosevelt

William Turner Levy

and

Cynthia Eagle Russett

John Wiley & Sons, Inc.

New York • Chichester • Weinheim • Brisbane • Singapore • Toronto

Copyright © 1999 by William Turner Levy, Victor Scherle, and Cynthia Eagle Russett. All rights reserved

Published by John Wiley & Sons, Inc.
Published simultaneously in Canada

The quotation on pages 131–132 from "A Masque of Reason" by Robert Frost is used with the generous permission of the copyright owner. From: "A Masque of Reason" in *The Poetry of Robert Frost*, edited by Edward Connery Lathem. Copyright 1945 by Robert Frost. © 1973 by Lesley Frost Ballantine. © 1969 by Henry Holt and Company, Inc. Reprinted by permission of Henry Holt and Company, Inc.

Frontispiece photograph is by Philippe Halsman, © Halsman Estate.

This publication is designed to provide accurate and authoritative information in regard to the subject matter covered. It is sold with the understanding that the publisher is not engaged in rendering professional services. If professional advice or other expert assistance is required, the services of a competent professional person should be sought.

Library of Congress Cataloging-in-Publication Data:
Levy, William Turner
    The extraordinary Mrs. R : a friend remembers Eleanor Roosevelt /
William Turner Levy, with Cynthia Eagle Russett.
        p.   cm.
    Includes index.
    ISBN 0-471-33177-5 (alk. paper)
        1. Roosevelt, Eleanor, 1884–1962. 2. Presidents' spouses—United
States Biography. 3. Roosevelt, Eleanor, 1884–1962—Friends and
associates. 4. Levy, William Turner.   I. Russett, Cynthia Eagle.
II. Title.
E807.1.R48L48   1999
973.917'092—dc21
    [B]   99-20989
                                                              CIP

Printed in the United States of America

10 9 8 7 6 5 4 3 2 1

Dedicated with love to
Robert J. and Kristin Dworkoski
—Bob and Kris—
who, like Mrs. R, have mastered
the art of friendship

Contents

A Note to the Reader

"We're going to have a party!" was the way Mrs. Roosevelt always greeted me once we had become fast friends and were about to embark on a notable evening, weekend, or longer time together. From her I learned the secret of the pursuit of happiness.

Victor Scherle, my friend and collaborator on two earlier books, with whom I often shared random memories of Mrs. Roosevelt, convinced me she came alive when I talked about her. The future, he allowed, was owed an account of my times with Mrs. Roosevelt. We spent many hours happily invoking her. The result was a manuscript that needed another's eye and thought. Cynthia Eagle Russett, a historian of modern America at Yale, graciously provided both. The order of the memories and the editorial matter that so adroitly connects them has been provided by Professor Russett. My debt to her skill, tact, and clarity is great.

In my agent, William B. Goodman, and my editor, Hana Umlauf Lane, I have been blessed with two champions of the profession of books. That they revered Mrs. Roosevelt as well gave working with them a simplicity and sureness rarely met.

William Turner Levy
Viewpoint School
Calabasas, California

Prologue

It was October 11, 1963.

Four-year-old Hall Delano Roosevelt, with his shock of bright red hair, pulled the cord and unveiled a poster-size reproduction of a five-cent commemorative stamp honoring his grandmother, Eleanor Roosevelt.

As I watched him, I remembered when he was barely two years old, learning to swim in the pool at Val-Kill Cottage. Now, on that day in October, his grandmother's birthday, he was standing as tall as possible, representing the Roosevelt family. All of her children were there to admire the purple oblong stamp featuring her radiantly smiling face. None could have foreseen that in the years ahead two more commemorative stamps would be issued to honor her, one on the one hundredth anniversary of her birth.

The postmaster general spoke briefly, introducing the president of the United States, John F. Kennedy, who also spoke briefly and then introduced Adlai E. Stevenson, who was likewise succinct.

The warmly informal ceremony took place in the Rose Garden of the White House. The green of the lawn, the whiteness of the house, and the colorful garb of several representatives of foreign nations added to the festive air.

The relatively small group of invited guests mingled and chatted. Now that a year had passed, we were no

President Kennedy, with James Roosevelt, in the Rose Garden at the White House on the occasion of the unveiling of the Eleanor Roosevelt postage stamp. *(Courtesy of William Turner Levy)*

longer in a mourning mood but a celebratory one. We each received a personally inscribed gold certificate bearing a block of four stamps canceled "First Day of Issue."

President Kennedy was all smiles, and, as he mingled with the guests, I noticed the red tinge in his sunlit hair for the first time.

Putting his arm around my shoulders, James Roosevelt led me into the White House to show me the oval office. When we returned to the Rose Garden a few minutes later, President Kennedy greeted us. Taking me aside, he clapped me on the shoulder and said, "What a great life. . . . What a great woman. . . . I envy you."

Chapter 1

An Invitation to Tea

PRESIDENT KENNEDY WAS RIGHT to envy William Turner Levy, who, in the last ten years of Eleanor Roosevelt's life, became one of her closest and dearest friends. They first met in the spring of 1953. At the time William Turner Levy was a young Episcopalian priest and faculty member in the English department at the City College of New York, his alma mater. He had written to Mrs. Roosevelt about his purchase of memorabilia from the collection of the late President Roosevelt and of his desire to learn more about some of the pieces. She, in response, had invited him to tea. It was the beginning of a friendship that lasted until her death.

৪৩৪

"WON'T YOU COME IN?" Eleanor Roosevelt said with a warm smile, raising her eyebrows delicately, and speaking in that distinctive, enthusiastic voice I had always known, but had never before heard directed to myself. She seized my hand in welcome.

1

A myriad of reactions and impressions distracted me as I followed Mrs. Roosevelt into her apartment in the Park Sheraton Hotel near Manhattan's Central Park. She was taller and bigger than I had imagined. She had a rich, beautifully toned voice, graceful movement and gestures, and a smile that was a reflection of her friendliness. Her step was light and swift. The woman striding in front of me was the most famous woman in the world. Soon I was to sit down with her over a cup of tea and "see her plain."

I was jarred out of further reverie by an unexpected sight in an adjoining bedroom: a portly lady in a slip, struggling with a garment she was pulling down over her head.

"Oh, do take a seat, Mr. Levy. I'll be right with you!" Mrs. Roosevelt announced abruptly, having caught the same sight that I had. She re-entered the living room almost immediately with the lady of the bedroom in tow.

"Hick, I want you to meet the Reverend William Turner Levy. Mr. Levy, this is my old friend, Miss Lorena Hickok."

"Well, hello!" Miss Hickok said exuberantly as she yanked at the skirt of her dress with one hand and quickly, necessarily, smoothed her hair with the other. "I've been trying on some dresses Mrs. Roosevelt has decided to part with—to see if any of them will fit me."

I liked Miss Hickok and her frankness at once, and after she had returned to the bedroom, Mrs. Roosevelt said to me, "Miss Hickok is an old friend, a newspaperwoman from the White House days, and I'm devoted to her. She says she won't have tea, but *we* will!" As she motioned me to a seat opposite her and reached for the teapot that was on a small table between us, I was acutely aware of the way in which her expressive voice and face and hands augmented her words. Her most ordinary statement reflected an impressive awareness of life. Tea was not a beverage—it was a friendly ritual between persons enthusiastic to be with each other.

My invitation to tea was occasioned by my recent purchase of a number of objects and books from the collection of the late President Franklin Delano Roosevelt and Mrs. Roosevelt. A public exhibition and sale had been held at New York's Hammer Galleries to benefit the National Foundation for Infantile Paralysis. I had written to Mrs. Roosevelt to say that I was enjoying the Rooseveltiana I had acquired, but that I would very much like to learn more about the history of some of the pieces, descriptions of which I enclosed.

So it was that on that early April afternoon in 1953 I found myself having tea with Eleanor Roosevelt.

"Will you tell me," Mrs. Roosevelt asked, invitingly, "about *yourself* and what you do?"

I told her that I was in my seventh year of teaching in the Department of English at the City College of New York, and that I was expecting to complete my doctorate at Columbia University in two months.

"English literature was always *my* favorite subject!" she interjected warmly, "and I *loved* teaching it at the Todhunter School in New York, though I'm sure it was at a very elementary level compared to your classes. I always taught the older girls," she added in a professional aside, "because there, I felt, my lack of teaching skill wouldn't matter as much! I continued my classes for a while after my husband and I moved into the White House, but regretfully had to give them up when there just wasn't enough time." She assumed an expression indicating that time was the inexorable enemy of her energetic capacities.

I regaled her with a few anecdotes about my teaching experiences and proceeded to explain that I was an Episcopal clergyman without a parish, a teaching clergyman. It had never been my intent to leave teaching when I decided to study at Union Theological Seminary.

"Isn't your combination a rare one?" Mrs. Roosevelt asked, half to herself, adding swiftly, "though I certainly see the value of the idea!"

"It is in this country," I replied, "but not in England, and I've been particularly encouraged by Dean [later Bishop] James A. Pike to help make it an American institution. It equips me better in my teaching of literature—from Milton to Eliot; and it also gives me a freedom to preach and do a somewhat less conventional parish ministry."

During tea, Mrs. Roosevelt told me all she knew about the books and objects I had purchased.

At one point she excused herself to take a telephone call. When she returned, she looked very sad. "Tommy—Malvina Thompson—is dying. She's not conscious and isn't likely to become so, but the doctors have promised to call me so that I can be with her at the end. I'm not going out or seeing anyone. But as you are a clergyman," she added, "I didn't mind seeing you."

I knew about Mrs. Roosevelt's more than thirty-year association with her secretary and friend and asked if there was anything I could do.

"Say a prayer for her tonight. Pray that she may go quickly."

Later, as I left the active, yet serene world of Eleanor Roosevelt and regretfully entered the noisy New York City street with its display of meaningless and wasted energy, I felt privileged to have met this enchanting lady, to have spent even so small a part of my life with her, for she was one who used time creatively and transcended the distractions of place.

But as I walked alone in Central Park, my gratitude for the experience was diabolically tempered by the realization that it was over. I envied those who called her friend and had this warming relationship always. I was ashamed of my envy, but it was painfully real, for at that time I believed that I would never have occasion to be with Mrs. Roosevelt again.

છ૭

At the time of this meeting, Eleanor Roosevelt was probably the best-known and most widely respected woman in the world. Although she had protested, after the death of her husband, that the story was over, in reality she had gone on to a life of global activism. In the years after World War II it was common for her to receive in a normal week over one hundred requests for public appearances. In 1946 President Truman appointed her to be one of five American delegates to the United Nations General Assembly meeting in London. As chair of the UN Human Rights Commission, she played a crucial role in the drafting of the Universal Declaration of Human Rights. It was no easy task, requiring determination and firmness tempered with wisdom and tolerance to marshal her fractious colleagues, especially those from the Soviet Union, into agreement. The result was a landmark achievement that UN Secretary-General U Thant called "the Magna Carta of mankind." Later, Mrs. Roosevelt would emphasize to William Turner Levy the document's critical role in raising the conscience of world governments: "You cannot talk about violation of human rights when there is no agreed definition of what those rights are!"

Despite his sad expectation that he would not see her again, William Turner Levy heard from Mrs. Roosevelt very soon after their first meeting, and they began to correspond. He would learn that amid all the distractions of celebrity, Eleanor Roosevelt remained a woman who gathered strength from close personal relationships. Though she and her husband, Franklin Delano Roosevelt, were devoted to each other and had an effective working partnership, their marriage had lacked the depths of romantic intimacy. As a result, Eleanor Roosevelt turned for solace to loving friendships with the men and women who were drawn to her throughout her life. She had, it was said, a profound gift for friendship, and she particularly enjoyed the company of younger people. "The people I love," she wrote to one friend, "mean more to me than all the public things. . . . I only do the public things because there are a few close people whom I love dearly and who matter to me above everything else." Though he could not know it in the spring of 1953, young William Turner Levy was to become one of those people whom Eleanor cherished, "above everything else."

That summer Eleanor Roosevelt introduced William Turner Levy to the hospitality of Val-Kill, the cottage on the Roosevelt property in Hyde Park that had become her retreat. Val-Kill was the place Eleanor Roosevelt loved above all others. The house itself was unpretentious—nothing like the big house in which Franklin Roosevelt had grown up, where Mrs. Roosevelt had never felt at home—but it had charm and warmth.

❧

A FEW DAYS AFTER our first meeting Mrs. Roosevelt wrote me: "I regret to have to tell you that Miss Thompson died yesterday afternoon." She had died eight years to the day after the President's death.

I wrote a letter of condolence and sent along a sermon that I had written on All Saints' Day. In reply, Mrs. Roosevelt wrote: "I want to thank you for your sweet note of sympathy and also for the sermon, which I liked very much. Miss Thompson was a devoted and loyal friend, as well as a great help to me in my work. I will miss her terribly."

Certain that Mrs. Roosevelt would find stimulation in the germinal ideas of Simone Weil on religion, politics, and education, I sent her *The Need for Roots*, marking her copy with notes from my own copy.

After that I began sending her clippings that I felt would interest her, particularly from British newspapers and periodicals to which I subscribed. On May 18, she wrote to say: "I shall be back, I hope, the second of August and shall hope to see you then." Referring to a second sermon I had sent her, she added in her unique, bold handwriting at the bottom of the typewritten letter, "I liked your sermon!"

Three days later, Mrs. Roosevelt left on an extensive fact-finding trip to Japan, Hong Kong, Istanbul, Athens, and Yugoslavia.

Newspaper reports noted that Mrs. Roosevelt was staying at the Imperial Hotel in Tokyo. I wrote to inform her that I had been awarded a doctor of philosophy degree in English by Columbia University. She replied on the engraved stationery of Frank Lloyd Wright's famous hotel on June 6, saying in part: "It is so nice to get news from home and I appreciate your thoughtfulness. . . . I congratulate you on your success and I fully realize what a fine feeling it is to have a difficult task finished."

In early August I wrote to welcome her home and mentioned that I was driving up to Hyde Park the following

Saturday to visit the Franklin D. Roosevelt home, gravesite, and library on a sort of annual trip. I was delighted
when she invited me to drive over to her house for tea on
that day.

Val-Kill Cottage, Mrs. Roosevelt's home at Hyde Park,
was located on a private road approximately two miles
back from "Springwood," the big Roosevelt house overlooking the Hudson. The cottage had originally been a
furniture factory, which Mrs. Roosevelt had set up during
the Depression in association with two friends. In an effort
akin to the Works Project Administration (WPA), local
artisans were employed to produce handmade reproduc-
tions of early American furniture. The factory was a two-
fold experiment: to determine whether a market existed
for relatively expensive quality furniture, and if so, to see
whether similar operations could be created to employ
skilled but unemployed workers across the country. The
hoped-for market did not materialize, and when the experiment was ended, Mrs. Roosevelt had the two-story building transformed into a cottage, with two living rooms, a
dining room, seven bedrooms, a sleeping dormitory for
young guests, two large screened porches downstairs, and a
screened sleeping porch upstairs. There was an attached
apartment for the couple who worked for her.

The cottage was located on Val-Kill Creek, which had
been dammed to create an attractive lake at that point.
There was a wooden bridge over the dam that made a
friendly clippity-clop sound as one drove across it. Nearby,
but before one reached Val-Kill Cottage, there was a stone
cottage occupied by Mrs. Roosevelt's youngest son, John,
and his family; the tennis courts and swimming pool were
located here, as well as a picnic area with a large stone bar-

becue. I first saw all this on that August day, when I went to the stone cottage by mistake and was greeted by Anne Roosevelt, who directed me to her mother-in-law's house.

Val-Kill Cottage, with its asymmetrical, cream-colored stucco exterior, was unprepossessing, but colorful flowers and sheltering trees of variety and beauty softened the building's severe lines. The necessary parking circle in front of the house (to accommodate Mrs. Roosevelt's many guests and visitors) was shaded by a splendid oak tree, with petunias planted at its base. Off the circle to the right of the house was a spacious one-room building of matching exterior, used as a rumpus room for youngsters on a rainy day, a retreat for a rained-out picnic group, or a dining room for state police and security officers who accompanied visiting heads of state.

Mrs. Roosevelt herself answered the door—with a radiant smile and an interested Scotty at her feet. She offered her hand in welcome, then turned briskly and, followed by her dog, led the way down a short hall into a large alcoved, wood-paneled living room furnished with the single purpose of being comfortable. This was the kind of room she chose to live in: The walls were covered with pictures—more photographs than paintings. The furniture was arranged so that people could be near each other and yet still have the light and convenience of a floor or table lamp and a side table. The objects on the fireplace mantle, the phonograph, the baby grand piano, and the many tables of various sizes were highly personal mementoes of a fully enjoyed life. Books in great number added the warmth of their presence and color.

I sat in one of the chairs fitted with a summery slipcover. Mrs. Roosevelt looked down at her Scotty, who had

Mrs. R was especially fond of Scotties. Here she is at Val-Kill in 1948 with Fala and Tamas. *(Courtesy of the Franklin D. Roosevelt Library)*

settled at her feet. "This is Mr. Duffy!" she exclaimed. "I call him 'Mister' because he's so dignified." She laughed and then pointed out a second Scotty, Tamas, who was half-hidden beneath the upholstery skirt of the chair next to me.

I asked the obvious question: "Is either one related to Fala?"

"Yes, Tamas is Fala's grandson. I'm afraid he hasn't been feeling too well lately. He *is* getting old!"

Indeed Tamas had many gray hairs. I leaned over and scratched him behind the ears, telling him that it was an honor to meet the grandson of President Roosevelt's illustrious dog.

Tamas perked up, looked at me, and was sufficiently complimented by my attention to waddle out from under the chair and sit closer to me. Mrs. Roosevelt smiled at both dogs affectionately. "They're very sweet. They even sleep on my bed at night. They have two beds of their own—from Abercrombie & Fitch, if you please—but do they sleep in them? No. They make themselves comfortable on *my* bed, and they poke their cold noses in my face every morning at dawn!" It was obvious that she considered this a great compliment.

At that moment, Mrs. Roosevelt's housekeeper carried in a silver tea service. Mrs. Roosevelt moved the low mahogany table that was alongside her chair to a position between us, raised the two drop leaves, which were surprisingly wide, and supported them with the gate legs. The tray was placed on this table.

Mrs. Roosevelt was wearing a cotton flowered-print dress in pastel colors. Her only jewelry was her wedding ring, her engagement ring, a silver wristwatch, and a small ruby ring on the little finger of her right hand.

The tea was Lapsang souchong, and there was a delicious huckleberry loaf cake. When I commented on the wonderful flavor of the huckleberries, Mrs. Roosevelt was gratified. "They are wild huckleberries and they come from Campobello Island, where we used to go summers.

I've always loved the wild cranberries and wild huckleberries and now I get them sent down in jars. I'm so glad you like them baked in cake!"

Above the nearby sofa on the wall opposite me was a reproduction of a Shoumatoff portrait of FDR and a framed poem in the large brush-stroke calligraphy of Lord Dunsany. I asked Mrs. Roosevelt about the poem.

"Good heavens, Mr. Levy," she said with an incredulous laugh, "you're the first person ever to have recognized that almost indecipherable script!"

She rose, lifted the poem from its nail, returned to her seat, and told me that she had been greatly touched when the Irish poet sent it to her. She read it aloud—an affecting memorial tribute to her husband.

As I replaced the poem on the wall for Mrs. Roosevelt, my eyes wandered to the left, to a modern Persian-style block-print wall hanging almost four feet square, made up of figures in stylized landscapes and several quotations, including the most famous lines from *The Rubáiyát of Omar Khayyám:* "Here, with a loaf of bread beneath the bough, a flask of wine, a book of verse—and thou beside me, singing in the wilderness—and wilderness is paradise enough."

Mrs. Roosevelt's voice rang out, interrupting my momentary reverie: "That wall hanging over the sofa you were looking at was created by an artist in one of the WPA projects. I've always thought it was particularly well conceived."

Before returning to my seat, I noticed that to the left of the wall hanging were two extremely valuable watercolors by Turner, the great nineteenth-century English painter.

The conversation, influenced by tea drinking and Dunsany, turned to England. Mrs. Roosevelt was fond of the

Lake District and we talked of Wordsworth's home, Dove Cottage. "When you were in the Lake District, did you see Ruskin's home at Lake Coniston?" Mrs. Roosevelt asked me.

"Only from the distance," I replied, "but even that was exciting."

Mrs. Roosevelt then led me over to the Turner watercolors. "These were given to Franklin as a boy by his godmother, Mrs. Blodgett. Her husband had known Ruskin," she said, pointing to a letter and engraved portraits of Ruskin and Turner. "In this letter framed here, Ruskin advises Mr. Blodgett to acquire these two watercolors, which are excellent examples of the earlier and later Turner styles."

After I was given an opportunity to absorb the almost startling beauty of beach and ship and cloud, Mrs. Roosevelt said, "Now let's go out on the porch—a breeze seems to have come up."

The screened porch off the living room, with its comfortable old-fashioned wicker furniture, was a perfect setting in which to relax on a summer day. It was an unadorned area, an interesting contrast to the room where we had just had tea.

The telephone rang in the living room and Mrs. Roosevelt excused herself to answer it. As I waited for her return, I reflected on the room I had just come from. It was most interesting for the photographs on the walls and side tables: at a glance I had recognized not only the President, who was Eleanor's distant cousin; the four Roosevelt sons; and the only daughter, Anna Roosevelt Halsted; but Elliott Roosevelt, Mrs. Roosevelt's father; his brother, Theodore Roosevelt; FDR's mother, Sara Delano Roosevelt; Louis

Was it something I said? This photo proves that even
Mrs. R could have a bad picture taken. The screened
porch off the living room at Val-Kill was a perfect place
for relaxing on a summer day. Here we are ensconced in
its comfortable wicker furniture. *(Courtesy of William
Turner Levy)*

Howe, his adviser and most intimate friend; and Lorena
Hickok, whom I had been introduced to when I first met
Mrs. Roosevelt. There were magnificent bronze and silver
inaugural medallions struck for each of the President's four
terms.

I had noticed over the fireplace a framed copy of the Roosevelt family crest, which consists of a silver shield with three red roses growing from a pleasant plot of green and the motto *"Qui Plantavit Curabit"* ("He who has planted it shall care for it"). The room was an eloquent testimony to the achievements, interests, and taste of its distinguished progenitor.

As Mrs. Roosevelt re-entered the porch, she said, "Mr. Levy, I'm chagrined to cut our delightful meeting short, but that telephone call reported an emergency that requires my immediate attention—a minor emergency, I suspect, but . . ." she sighed and elevated her eyebrows in her characteristically expressive way.

It couldn't have been a more gracious dismissal. And I hastened to say I had a wonderful time.

Chapter 2

Mrs. Roosevelt Comes to Dine

As they grew better acquainted, William Turner Levy sought to reciprocate Eleanor Roosevelt's hospitality. He invited her to dine with his parents and himself at their home in Riverdale, the Bronx, New York.

William Turner Levy's father, Jacob Levy, was a self-made man who rose from humble origins to become president of a well-known second-generation firm of New York stevedores, M. P. Smith and Sons, and was comfortably retired. Jacob Levy and Florence Agnes Turner, also a New Yorker, had married when they were in their thirties. William Turner Levy was their adopted son.

♣

After being Mrs. Roosevelt's guest on at least four occasions, I invited Mrs. Roosevelt for dinner at my home. I felt that to be in awe and not do so would be to do less for Mrs. Roosevelt than I would for any other new friend. She replied with her usual promptness: "I'd love to come. Do have your mother write to me."

Together with my parents, Jacob Levy and Florence
Turner Levy. Mrs. R was often a guest at our home in
Riverdale. *(Courtesy of William Turner Levy)*

Mrs. Roosevelt replied promptly to the dates my
mother offered.

On the day before, I telephoned Maureen Corr, her
secretary, to ask her about Mrs. Roosevelt's preferences in
food.

"How kind of you to inquire, Dr. Levy. Mrs. Roosevelt
eats and enjoys everything!"

"Please tell me then, Miss Corr, will Mrs. Roosevelt
have a drink before dinner, and, if so, what does she like to
drink?"

"Mrs. Roosevelt doesn't care much about drinking, but
if the other people are drinking she'll have tomato juice or
maybe a glass of sherry."

"What other people?" I asked in panic. "There's only to be my parents and myself, as my mother wrote Mrs. Roosevelt at the time of the original invitation."

"Really? How wonderful for Mrs. Roosevelt! I know Mrs. Levy wrote that, but people often do, you know, and then when the time comes they find they can't resist inviting relatives and few close friends—to show off Mrs. Roosevelt!"

I told Miss Corr that if my parents and I were considering having a large dinner party we would have asked Mrs. Roosevelt whom she would like us to invite.

"Well, Dr. Levy, I must tell Mrs. Roosevelt that she's in for a rare treat, a quiet, relaxing dinner of the sort she hopes for but almost never gets! I do think, under the circumstances, that if you and your parents have a drink before dinner she'd probably love a sherry!"

As THE CLOCK WAS STRIKING SEVEN on the evening of January 19, the apartment doorbell rang. My mother went to the door, followed by my father and myself, and there stood Mrs. Roosevelt on her first visit to our home. It was an entirely different sensation—a supreme compliment—to have *her* as *our* guest!

Mrs. Roosevelt had been escorted to our door by her chauffeur, William White, who, now that the door had been opened, promptly turned and walked back to the elevator. "He will pick me up later, when I phone him," she explained to my mother, as she stepped into the apartment to be greeted by my father and me.

Mrs. Roosevelt was wearing a dark blue brocade evening coat adorned with practical black fur cuffs that could be used as a muff. Her red fingernails and brocade wrap gave her an air reminiscent of the Orient. Her gray hair was worn extremely short in the attractive, popular style called a feather cut. I helped her off with her coat and saw that she was wearing a black lace floor-length dinner dress.

While I hung her wrap in the hall closet, my father and mother led her to my book-lined study, where we were to have our drinks. By the time I reached the study, she was comfortably seated on a small sofa with my mother. She looked so wonderfully relaxed that it was difficult to believe she had returned from a demanding trip only the day before.

Mrs. Roosevelt accepted a glass of sherry; my mother, father, and I had bone-dry gin martinis. I was particularly gratified when I saw how much Mrs. Roosevelt enjoyed the pâté de foie gras, which I had suggested we serve. Indeed, before long, because it was on the Vermont marble cocktail table near her, Mrs. Roosevelt was serving *us* the pâté!

Mrs. Roosevelt volunteered that she knew exactly where we lived in Riverdale—a short distance north of the Henry Hudson Bridge, overlooking the Hudson River and the New Jersey Palisades—because "Once, when Franklin was president, he and I drove up here to visit Ed Flynn, the longtime county Democratic leader of the Bronx. He lived in the apartment house just south of you."

"Do you mean the Hudson Gardens apartment?" my mother asked.

"Yes, that's it," Mrs. Roosevelt replied. "They were on the top floor like you. It was really a house built on top of the apartment building and had its own private elevator."

Mrs. Roosevelt then changed the subject. "Tell me about your drapes," she asked, "Are they Don Quixote and Sancho Panza?" She appeared delighted at that prospect.

I told her they were. "They're done from drawings by Salvador Dalí."

She rose to examine them more closely. The lamp on my desk at the window illuminated them perfectly and she pulled one section of the drape out to see the entire design. "I think they're absolutely perfect—especially for this room!" Then, pointing to the books, and mentioning the books from floor to ceiling in the entrance hall, she added, "I never know what to think when I go into a house without books!"

On the wall opposite the sofa was a Dalí etching of the Crucifixion in a gold frame. She walked over to examine it before resuming her seat. "I'm not certain that I like all that Dalí does, but *this* is intriguing." Like a similar painting in Glasgow, Scotland, it presented an unusual view of the crucified Christ: from above.

"What do you think the unusual angle means?" Mrs. Roosevelt, now seated, asked me.

"I think of it as God's view of the event," I replied. "I must tell you that one day I saw Dalí alone on Madison Avenue. He seemed not to be in a hurry, so I stopped him for a moment and introduced myself and my mother, who was with me. He was interested when Mother mentioned our having this etching. 'Ah,' he said, his eyes brightening, 'the crucifixion of mine at the Metropolitan Museum of Art—where the Christ is not attached to the cross—is the vision of St. John of the Cross; the Glasgow Crucifixion—' he said with a dramatic farewell flourish, 'that is the vision of Salvador Dalí!'"

Mrs. Roosevelt was much amused.

Also on the wall was a mahogany Val-Kill miniature bookcase I had bought at the Hammer Galleries sale. FDR had housed his miniature book collection in this. Mrs. Roosevelt smiled, noticing it, and said, "I recognized it the minute I walked in. I'm so glad you have some of his best books!"

Just then my mother announced that dinner was ready. When we were seated at the dining table next to the windows, I said grace and we began our meal, which consisted of tomato soup, broiled steak, baked potatoes, corn on the cob, Brussels sprouts, celery and black olives, stewed fruit with English biscuits, and large coffees.

The dark red drapes—medieval figures against a *mille fleurs* background—covered the entire wall of windows. Candles lighted the table, including the centerpiece, a brilliant red cyclamen plant in a crystal bowl. Once again, I noted Mrs. Roosevelt's hearty appetite, and the beauty and animation of her face, whether she was speaking or listening. I knew she was having a good time. The soft light reflected warmly off her pearls: one long strand of large pearls and a second necklace made up of three strands of small pearls joined every six inches by diamond clasps. At the neckline of her black lace dress was a small diamond fleur-de-lys, which had been, I somehow knew, an important early gift from her husband. After her twelve years of intense exposure in the White House, the public knew a great many personal details about "The First Lady of the World."

Dinner was served by Frank, a waiter, whom we had come to know from frequent dining at the Barclay Hotel in New York. We had asked him to serve because we wanted to spend as much of our time with Mrs. Roosevelt as possible. Also, we knew that Frank, an outspoken admirer of President Roosevelt, would cherish this opportunity.

My mother, Florence Turner Levy, loved to accommodate Mrs. R's considerable appetite by serving her favorite dishes. *(Courtesy of William Turner Levy)*

To my delight, Mrs. Roosevelt had easily cleaned her dessert plate and accepted a second portion. "This is something I very rarely do," she said, "and oughtn't to do, for my weight's sake!" We enjoyed the compliment, and so did Frank, who served her generously.

At the table, Mrs. Roosevelt was taken with a silver Victorian dinner bell in the form of a turtle. It could be rung by depressing either the head or tail. Mrs. Roosevelt ran her finger over it lightly several times and said, "I'm using one of my mother's that isn't loud enough. This is wonderfully loud!" My mother showed her how to wind it from the bottom. Once, when Frank was in the room,

Mrs. Roosevelt couldn't resist trying it out! It seemed to her a "sensible" dinner bell.

Mrs. Roosevelt said, "I wonder if I might use your telephone. I have to let William know at what time you expect me to leave!"

I said, "Never!" She laughed.

My father said that he would consider it a privilege to drive her home whenever she had to leave, and that way we might prolong the pleasure of her visit. She readily agreed and telephoned to tell William that she would not require him anymore that night as "Mr. Levy has kindly offered to drive me home later."

Mother indicated a large armchair as one Mrs. Roosevelt might find comfortable. She seated herself in it and we circled ourselves around her as Frank finished clearing the table. She admired a pink azalea on the table next to her chair and then spoke of her chauffeur. She told us that William was the brother of Josh White, the American blues singer, and he himself used to sing. "He came to me after the war saying he wouldn't sing again and asked for work. I told him he wouldn't like servant's work, but he begged to be tried." She smiled with tolerant amusement, and added that he treated all of her guests as if they were *his* friends. She appeared to find him remarkable, too. "You know, he serves his brother when Josh White visits me and is entirely at ease!"

Mrs. Roosevelt recalled another one of her servants, Irene (she pronounced her name in the European fashion with three syllables), who once scorched a shirt of Franklin Jr.'s, whereupon she packed her bags and prepared to leave because of this terrible misdemeanor. Irene's European background had been terrifying. Her husband had died in a concentration camp and she herself had suffered terribly there. "I had to sit her down and talk plainly about how she was distressing me. 'It is true that we value possessions because they remind us of a happy time or of a person we love, but persons are more—infinitely more—important!' I told her. 'And it's unkind of you to distress me by thinking that I value or could value anything I own more than your peace of mind.'" Once again, throughout the telling of this incident, the earnest, serious Eleanor Roosevelt was revealed.

Mrs. Roosevelt then enjoyed telling us a story from her childhood. On warm summer days at her grandparents' summer home in Tivoli, where she lived on the Hudson River north of Hyde Park after her mother's death, she would read all day in a tree. She was then eight years old. Of course she had to admit when she returned to the house late in the day, having missed lunch, that she had lost track of time. Mrs. Roosevelt more acted out than told this story, the mock-innocent look on her face aiding her shaking head and the inflection of her voice.

Even as a child, Mrs. Roosevelt had loved reading. "But on Sundays," she said, "I had to put aside any book I was reading, regardless of how caught up I was in the story, and read a 'suitable' book. What I used to do, I'm afraid, is hide the book I was reading under my mattress and then go up to my room and dig it out and read it instead of the pious volume provided!" She was not one to look forward to Sundays in her strict grandparents' home, she said. Her grandfather was so theologically minded "that he kept a resident clergyman in the house so that he had someone to discuss theology with! On Sundays I had to go to church twice, morning and evening. I can still feel the jolts of riding there in a cart! And my grandparents' attitude made the day gloomy no matter how brightly the sun shone."

My father, whose childhood religious training also evoked unpleasant memories, told her he knew exactly what she meant. We soon got to talking about President Roosevelt's churchgoing habits in the last years. Mrs. Roosevelt explained, "My husband didn't go to church much then because he found it too painful to put the braces on. They were *terrible*! And also, he didn't like the fact that so many Secret Service men had to accompany him." Each year on the anniversary of his inauguration he had the clergy hold a special service in the White House. "I think it shows the confidence that the people had in Franklin that there was never a word of protest against his having religious services in the President's house."

My mother excused herself and went into the kitchen, sensing that Frank was getting ready to leave. She returned and asked Mrs. Roosevelt if Frank might say good-bye to her and if she would autograph a photograph of his eight-year-old daughter for her. Mrs. Roosevelt readily consented. Flustered and shy, Frank dug the photograph out of his wallet and I gave Mrs. Roosevelt a pen. "She's a beautiful child," Mrs. Roosevelt told him. "I hope she grows up to have a happy and useful life." Frank all but backed out of the room.

My father asked Mrs. Roosevelt about Secretary of State Dulles, with whom she had worked in the UN. "Dulles is too blunt," she replied. "He insults people without knowing it—he's *very* insensitive. When I was in Israel I was told that he presented Ben-Gurion with a leather-bound copy of the Bible—including the New Testament!"

This led my father to ask how she reacts to the venom of men like the journalist Westbrook Pegler. "In the case of Mr. Pegler himself, I must say I feel sorry for him," she replied. "His hatred of the Roosevelts is a disease. It must preoccupy him. Imagine waking up in the morning and knowing that you will spend a good part of the day thinking about people you loathe!"

The conversation shifted to her abundant daily mail. I asked if much of it was vilifying.

"Some. I answer a correspondent who seems genuinely confused three times and then I stop. If by that time you can't clarify matters, then nothing you say will make any difference. At the moment, I understand, my biography is being written by a vilifier!" She paused a moment and added, "I had a letter the other day that read: 'How *dare* you show your face after the monstrous things that went on in the White House between Harry Hopkins and your husband!' This goes on because I will never sue anyone, and they know it."

I asked Mrs. Roosevelt if she knew Walt Kelly's comic strip or the books he was writing about his character Pogo. She said she had never heard of Pogo. I brought her a copy of *The Pogo Papers* from a nearby bookshelf. She put on her glasses and read a short satirical section I pointed out on a character who closely resembled the notorious Senator Joseph McCarthy, then at the height of his iniquity. Her admiring comment was, "There's something *to* this. I will be on the lookout for your friend Pogo!"

It was twenty minutes to eleven and we reluctantly suggested that she might like to leave, as it would take at least a half hour for her to reach home. She rose, said she had had a marvelous evening, and agreed that it was time for her to depart.

On the drive to her home, Mrs. Roosevelt sat in the back seat with my mother, and at one point held her hand.

The drive was an enjoyment for Mrs. Roosevelt, too, and she liked seeing once again the twinkling lights on the George Washington Bridge. "When I go for a drive in the country," Mrs. Roosevelt said, chuckling, "I sit in front with the chauffeur and the two dogs sit in the back seat! Can you imagine what the neighbors must say!"

My mother kissed Mrs. Roosevelt good night, my father shook her hand, and I took her to the front door of her duplex garden apartment in a converted New York brownstone. She had moved from the Park Sheraton Hotel to this quiet tree-lined street on the East Side of Manhattan several months before.

"I feel revivified," Mrs. Roosevelt said, taking my hand in both of hers. "Thank you *ever* so much!"

ON ANOTHER OCCASION when Mrs. Roosevelt came to dinner, my mother surprised her with broiled scallops, a favorite of Mrs. Roosevelt's. After dinner, Mrs. Roosevelt took time to examine some of the poems and photographs framed on our walls. I recall that she particularly admired the "L'Envoi" to Padraic Colum's *Verses for Alfeo Faggi's Stations of the Cross*, written out in his own hand:

> Prince, by thine own darkened hour,
> Live within me, heart and brain;
> Let my hands not slip the rein!

> Ah, how long ago the hour
> Since a comrade rode with me:
> Now, a moment, let me see

> Thyself, lonely in the dark,
> Perfect, without wound nor mark!

We often had hors d'oeuvres in my study before dinner, and Mrs. R was always glad to lend a hand in serving. *(Courtesy of William Turner Levy)*

and a typed copy of a prayer inscribed "To William Turner Levy, with affection and respect, Reinhold Niebuhr":

> Our Father: Have mercy upon us for appropriating so rich a life with so little concern for those to whom beauty and joy are denied, whether by the cruelties of nature, the inhumanities of men or by their own limitations. Since we are debtors both to the wise and the unwise, teach us to discharge our debts to those who have given us much by serving those who need us greatly. In all things subject us to the spirit and the mind of Christ in whose name we pray. Amen.

We had acquired finger bowls and adopted their use for our guest's greater comfort. To be able to pace the dinner exactly to the mood of the evening and to provide a complete sense of privacy, we had determined never again to have anyone serve dinner when Mrs. Roosevelt came; on those occasions, I would enjoy the privilege myself. Mrs. Roosevelt, having been told, said she very much appreciated the idea, and she suggested that after dinner it would be fun for my mother and her to do the dishes together! Only the presence of a dishwasher convinced her that this was not necessary.

Over after-dinner coffee, pieces of bittersweet chocolate, and crystalized ginger, Mrs. Roosevelt told us some memorable stories. The Niebuhr prayer had made her think of the dire poverty she had seen in 1933, and in particular of a visit to West Virginia. "One of the homes I visited, a company house in a mining district, had a family with six children. When I was invited in—you see, I was with one of the Quaker social workers in the area, and not yet a recognized face—I was appalled at the hopelessness that you just *felt*. The husband was working, but the wage was totally inadequate because there wasn't that much work. His wife looked exhausted—largely, I suspected, because of inadequate diet. On the table was a bowl of what I can only call scraps, the sort of thing we would throw to a dog, and that was the midday meal." Mrs. Roosevelt tensed her entire body, leaned forward, and continued: "The children were obviously frightened of strangers, but as I was leaving I noticed that one little boy was clutching a white rabbit to his chest. He was just too shy to really show him to me, but I walked a step closer and told him what a handsome fellow the rabbit was! He smiled then, and clutched it even more protectively. Suddenly, his sister, thin and scrawny, looked at her brother in a hateful, mean way. Then she turned and said to me with cruel emphasis, 'He thinks we're not going to eat it, but we *are*!' And at that the boy fled down the road with the rabbit. One couldn't really blame the little girl when one saw the conditions under which they were forced to live. That is what poverty, real hunger, reduces us to!"

It was evident that the encounter had burned itself into Mrs. Roosevelt's mind. The passage of time and the projects she had worked on, which had relieved the worst conditions in the area, never obliterated her memory of the dehumanizing effects of want.

That evening she also related an illuminating story about Sara Delano Roosevelt. "It was one of the cruelest things I have ever heard of," she told us. "When Franklin's mother's closest friend, who had been her girlhood chum as well, ran away from her husband with another man, or so it was said, Franklin's father forbade his wife ever to see her again! When a letter would come, he would give it to his wife and have her burn it unopened before his eyes! It was a terrible sadness for her, but, of course, in those days, your husband's word was absolute law. So she never knew the true circumstances of her friend's actions. 'As far as you are concerned,' James Roosevelt told his wife, 'she is dead, and you are never to bring up her name again.'" Mrs. Roosevelt added one observation: "I know that if my husband had ever been that unreasonable, I should *not* have obeyed him, and should have told him why I wouldn't."

Mrs. Roosevelt noticed on my desk the silver frame I had had Tiffany make for the wartime snapshot of her husband that she had given me. She picked it up and read the engraving on the top, "The President, 1943" and on the bottom, "From Eleanor Roosevelt" in a facsimile of her signature. "I am *so* glad you like it so much," was her quiet comment, as she patted me on the shoulder.

That spurred me to show her one of the volumes from my collection of her husband's miniature books: a beautifully boxed, but well-worn copy of the New Testament in French. She turned to the inscription page, and read the faded ink: "Eleanor A. Roosevelt, *souvenir du printemps de* 1896, L.H.L., New York."

"I was eleven then," she remarked brightly, "and look at these pencil marks of mine." She showed them to us in the text. "Those are the passages I had to memorize for my French tutor. 'L.H.L.' stands for Mlle. Le Clerq, but I can't remember her first names, if, indeed, I ever knew them!"

She turned to the thirteenth chapter of the First Epistle to the Corinthians and read in impeccable French the portion on charity, *caritas*, beginning, "When I was a child I spoke like a child, . . ." "*Quand j'étais enfant, je parlais comme un enfant. . . . Maintenant donc ces trois demeurent; la foi, l'espérance et la charité; mais la plus grande est la charité.*"

She put the book back into its protective slipcase, and I saw by her expression that she was amused by its careful preservation. "How I sweated over that book!" she recalled. "And you gave it to your husband for his collection?" I inquired. "Yes, would you like me to add that?" she asked, removing the book once again as I extended a desk pen. She wrote, "Given by me to F.D.R., E.R." under the original inscription. "That was Franklin's favorite passage," she mused aloud, "and did you know he had the old Dutch family Bible opened to it for each of his inaugurations as governor and president?"

We looked at two other books, one a German yearbook of 1784, with a full account and many engravings of the American Revolution. It contained the first color copy of the American flag ever to appear in a book; portraits of Washington and Franklin and John Paul Jones, all still alive; and one of the earliest maps of the new nation, indicating as useful information where the Sioux might be found and extensive meadows full of buffalos!

"Franklin considered this an important book," Mrs. Roosevelt told us, and when I showed her a 1521 Aldus Press copy of the comedies of Terence signed by the President and annotated, "Bought by me in Venice in 1905—very fine copy," she exclaimed, "*That* was on our honeymoon! Franklin was always disappearing for hours in old bookstores." Then she remembered: "He took a course at Harvard in which he read Terence."

When we drove Mrs. Roosevelt home I went in with her and waited a moment while she lit several lights. Then I kissed her good night and said, "That was a terrible story about your mother-in-law having to give up her best friend!"

"I've always been horrified by it," Mrs. Roosevelt rejoined. "It's not a way we could live." She looked at me intently. "Two years before my marriage to Franklin I decided I wanted to live alone. Everyone was opposed to the idea. It was *unthinkable*. I should lose my reputation. I went to Auntie Bye, my Uncle Ted's sister, whose mind was like a man's—a man with a good mind—and I told her what I proposed to do. She said to me, 'You will never be able to please everyone. Do what you want if you are convinced that it is something you could tell someone you love—and who loves you—without shame!' I have always lived by that."

❧❧❧

Over time, Mrs. Roosevelt became fond of William Turner Levy's parents, visiting them at their home on many occasions

*and including them in invitations to dinner and the theater.
She even grew fond of the family cat, Lord Peter Wimsey.*

*When William's father died following a stroke, Mrs. Roosevelt broke her longstanding rule about not attending funerals
and slipped unobtrusively into the church to be with his mother.*

⌘

AN INVITATION FROM Mrs. Roosevelt began, "Is there any Broadway show you and your mother and father would like to see, and would you all be free on the evening of Tuesday, November twenty-second? If you can choose one, I will try to get the tickets, and I would love to have you dine with me this time at the Cosmopolitan Club. You have always given me a party, and this year I would like to give it for your father and mother."

When I informed Mrs. Roosevelt that my mother's and father's birthdays were on November 12 and 15, respectively, she was delighted with this coincidence, which added further color to the theater party.

On the evening of November 22, we had a "party" indeed, to use a favorite word of Mrs. Roosevelt's! She and my mother looked truly festive in contrasting lavender and beige evening gowns. After a splendid steak dinner at the Cosmopolitan Club, we all enjoyed the folksy hilarity of Ira Levin's play *No Time for Sergeants*. Andy Griffith was a new talent, perfectly cast as the hillbilly private who found himself the creator of absurd situations by his mere innocence. The scenes between this ingenuous private and the Army brass, particularly the Army psychiatrist, were tellingly done and the mirth was greatly enhanced by the fine acting of Myron McCormick and Roddy McDowall. The play had actually been my father's choice, and we were all happy that he had so decided.

Later that evening, in Mrs. Roosevelt's living room, after birthday toasts to my parents, my father spoke of his unswerving confidence in President Truman's election in 1948. Mrs. Roosevelt admitted that she was surprised by the unexpected victory. She asked my father what had made him so confident.

"I ignored all the campaign talk on both sides," he revealed. "The important thing was that the economic picture was excellent, everyone had more money than before, business was very good, and Wall Street confident. Unless there was a major issue to override these facts, I didn't believe a president would be turned out of the White House in a time of prosperity. The voter is finally alone with himself in the voting booth, and he thinks, 'I'm well off, better off than I've been for years, so why risk upsetting the apple cart?'"

Mrs. Roosevelt agreed that it was a just analysis, "as the result proved. I think some of us were thinking about too many things at once and missing the main point. Oh," she added with a chuckle, "wasn't it a *glorious* day!"

My father recalled: "I'll never forget how the Dewey forces, faced with continued losses, kept saying, through the course of that night and early morning, 'Wait till the rural vote comes in!' and when it did, it went to Truman, too!"

I had brought with me an endearing letter that I had recently received from Dorothy Canfield Fisher, and that I knew Mrs. Roosevelt would enjoy reading:

You just have an intuition as to when some special gesture is needed by one of your circle. Why wouldn't you begin to have that intuition, young as you are (or as you seem to this ancient Vermont friend), giving as much advice as you constantly do to those who need it?

One of the trials of being pretty well on in one's seventies is that there is an occasional ebb of the tide, leaving the old beach pretty bare and cheerless. It was at just such a moment that you came in with the flood tide of appreciation and warm friendliness, which made me (and this is the best thing one can say for anybody's health) look around me to see really the greatness of the sea and the radiance of the sun, and that I have my share of them. Thank you so much.

"Intuition . . ." Mrs. Roosevelt looked up and said the word thoughtfully. Then, handing the letter back to me, she asked that I read it aloud. The word, and the sense of the letter, struck me more forcibly when I looked at my parents' faces and fully realized what Mrs. Roosevelt had achieved with her "party." She had accomplished what she had set out to do—she had rendered two human beings supremely happy. A sense of profound gratitude overwhelmed me.

MRS. ROOSEVELT'S VISITS weren't always meticulously planned in advance. One morning when my mother was confined to bed with a particularly virulent attack of flu, the telephone rang and Mrs. Roosevelt asked, "May I stop by for just five minutes? I've some roses from Hyde Park— they're so lovely and cheering!"

Two hours later the doorman rang our apartment. "Mrs. Roosevelt asks if she can come up."

Mrs. Roosevelt rang the doorbell just minutes later. She handed me the brilliant roses after we greeted each other, and I followed her swift strides to my mother's corner bedroom.

"Florence, dear," Mrs. Roosevelt said in greeting, "these are six of John's quail." (Her son, and next-door

Along with myself, my mother was often invited to Hyde Park to spend weekends at Val-Kill. Here we are with Mrs. R strolling the grounds of the Presidential Library. *(Courtesy of William Turner Levy)*

neighbor at Hyde Park, raised quail as a hobby.) Mrs. Roosevelt continued, "To pique your appetite. And aren't these *huge* grapes? Black, seedless, and so sweet, and Marge, my housekeeper, you know, sent along some of her just-baked lemon butter cookies. I know you'll take good care of yourself and so be up in no time! Now I'm off to a rather dull meeting, I fear. Tubby's waiting for me downstairs." Tubby was her driver at that time.

She was gone with a cheerful wave and that glorious warm smile, leaving the bedroom in a glow—and my quickly recovering mother all smiles.

ONE MARCH 17, although I knew Mrs. Roosevelt was not at home, I stopped by her town house apartment to drop off a small pot of shamrocks flown in from Eire for the occasion. It was also the anniversary of her marriage. Franklin and Eleanor Roosevelt had been married on St. Patrick's Day because it was on that day that President Theodore Roosevelt, who gave his niece away, was to be in New York to attend the parade. She had once laughingly told me, "We were certainly upstaged that day—at our own wedding! Not that Franklin and I minded finding ourselves all alone as the guests flocked around the president!"

Two days later, anticipating an upcoming visit to our home, she wrote, "It will be fun to meet your Lord Peter Wimsey!" Our family cat, Judy, had recently died and we had immediately acquired a female kitten, which my mother, ignoring the kitten's sex, had named Lord Peter Wimsey after the detective hero she admired in Dorothy L. Sayers' mystery novels.

"Roast duck with orange sauce!" was Mrs. Roosevelt's delighted exclamation at dinner the following week. It was an evening that now took on a "traditional" pattern of delights, thanks to repetition. There was even time for music, and I introduced Mrs. Roosevelt, through British recordings, to several of the great moments in Elgar's magnificent oratorio, *The Dream of Gerontius*, based on Cardinal Newman's poem.

Mrs. Roosevelt had observed in my parents' bedroom a small oval painting on ivory of the Taj Mahal, and over drinks before dinner, she spoke of its personal significance to her.

Her father had told her about the Taj Mahal. "He had found it to be the one unforgettable thing he had seen in India, and he vowed that we would see it together." She, of course, loved to do things with her father—had looked into the crater of Mount Vesuvius while holding onto his strong hand. "But it was a promise he didn't live to keep," Mrs. Roosevelt told us wistfully. "We were not to have a life together, and I suppose I have always felt, because I loved him so deeply, that I missed a part of my life that was promised me as a child."

In *India and the Awakening East*, Mrs. Roosevelt described her first sight of the great tomb Shah Jehan built for his Persian wife, Mumtaz Mahal, fulfilling a pledge to make her name live forever:

> As we came through the entrance gallery into the walled garden and looked down the long series of oblong pools in which the Taj and the dark cypresses are reflected, I held my breath, unable to speak in the face of so much beauty. The white marble walls, inlaid with semi-precious stones, seemed to take on a mauve tinge with the coming night, and about halfway along I asked to be allowed to sit down on one of the stone benches and just look at it. The others walked on, but I felt that this first time I wanted to drink in its beauty from a distance. One does not want to talk and one cannot glibly say this is a beautiful thing, but one's silence, I think, says this is a beauty that enters the soul. With its minarets rising at each corner, its dome and tapering spire, it creates a sense of airy, almost floating lightness; looking at it, I decided I had never known what perfect proportions were before.

The rest of the passage, too, is so informed with perceptive observation that I had used it in teaching descriptive writing, a fact which pleased its author. It was mind-boggling to us both that, had he lived, Shah Jehan would have built an exact mirror-image tomb for himself—but in black!

THAT SAME EVENING, admiring my mother's hand-painted and signed Spode dessert plates and demitasses, copies of eighteenth-century Spode originals, Mrs. Roosevelt talked of her grandmother's care for her heirloom dessert set. She would have the maids bring a basin of soapy water and one of hot, clear rinsing water right to the table and proceed to wash these treasures herself. "We would think it strange today," Mrs. Roosevelt said, rather in awe of such individuality.

Lord Peter Wimsey had been an instant success. I read a letter to Mrs. Roosevelt from T. S. Eliot in which he condoled with me on the recent death of our cat, Judy, but rejoiced in the knowledge that we had acquired a successor (Lord Peter Wimsey), adding that he believed the best cats were of obscure origin. He felt that pedigree cats were no good, stupid, nervous, and of feeble character, whereas the common cat was likely to be a cat of strong character.

Mrs. Roosevelt was delighted with Tom's forthrightness. Tom and Wimsey had become fast friends, Tom even inquiring, "Is Wimsey there?" during a transatlantic telephone call. Indeed, he even addressed us in one letter: "Dear Florence, Jack, William & Wimsey." Once, alluding to his volume of cat poems, *Old Possum's Book of Practical Cats* (Eliot was dubbed "Old Possum" by Ezra Pound), Tom greeted his friend, waiting at the apartment door: "Ah, Lord Peter Wimsey, it's your Uncle Tom Possum!" Wimsey reacted by rolling on her back and leaping to a chair. Tom said, "You're a very *acrobatic* cat—but are you a *practical* cat?"

Mrs. Roosevelt's friendship with Wimsey also grew. Indeed, we of the household were always aware that Wimsey, in justifiable pride, had no trouble holding her tail perpendicular.

PASCAL, IN *pensée* number 382, triumphantly defines the power of one individual to make a difference. When Mrs. Roosevelt told me that until she met Wimsey she really had no feeling for cats, I was certain that Pascal would have been impressed by Wimsey.

Wimsey certainly made a difference in our family. When my mother, in her seventies, broke her leg climbing a mountaintop trail in Vermont, it resulted in her only hospitalization in a ninety-year lifetime. So that she would not be, God forbid, "catless," I found a wonderfully appealing Italian pottery cat, naturalistic and lifesize, at a favorite shop of hers on Park Avenue. Later, when Mrs. Roosevelt came to know us, she would sometimes stop to chuck the ceramic cat under the chin or pat it on the head—all a result of Wimsey's potent influence. Once she said to my mother, "How could one ever feel blue with that around!" Then Mrs. Roosevelt remembered that there was a beautiful porcelain cat, also lifesize, sitting near the piano in Springwood, the Roosevelt home in Hyde Park. "Wouldn't it be wonderful if I could borrow it for my home? I live far too hectic a life to accommodate a flesh-and-blood cat!"

Little did Mrs. Roosevelt know that lots of red tape would have to be cut before she could achieve this simple goal. She discovered, she told us in reporting on the ongoing saga, that it was unprecedented for a private citizen to receive a loan from a national historic site! But she persisted. She was persuasive. A compromise was reached. She would lend an even more valuable Roosevelt heirloom to the National Parks Service in return. Documents were drawn up and finally all necessary signatures affixed!

"Well, Wimsey," she addressed our cat with a laugh, "you certainly started me on what I began to fear was a wild goose chase, but, fortunately for the outcome, I discovered that several of the officials involved are cat lovers!" Wimsey, though noncommittal, was remarkably attentive.

Writing to Lord Peter Wimsey on October 12, 1961, the day after the last birthday Mrs. Roosevelt was well enough to celebrate, she said: "It was most kind and thoughtful of you to remember my birthday and I would like to thank you warmly for your card and the very lovely handkerchief. You must be the world's kindest cat!"

That December, Mrs. Roosevelt's last Christmas, she again addressed her favorite cat:

> There are all kinds of cats, I know, but you are the only one who remembers special occasions. I'm greatly flattered that you pamper me with Hartnell's "In Love" and I cannot thank you enough. Your taste is most discriminating, but then I know you love to preen!
>
> With appreciation from
Eleanor Roosevelt.

AFTER HIS STROKE, my father was unconscious during his month-long stay at New York's Saint Luke's Hospital. Mrs. Roosevelt shared our anxieties, and then our grief at his death. Although we were aware that Mrs. Roosevelt attended only family funerals because of the vast number she would have to attend as the result of her husband's and her own public life, she explained this to us again. "I will pray for the repose of his soul," she said, feelingly.

Late on the night before the service at All Angels Episcopal Church, Mrs. Roosevelt telephoned. "William, would it mean a great deal to your mother if I came tomorrow?" I answered her at once: "Yes, it would."

"I do not wish to attract any attention," she said. "Is there a side entrance I can slip in through and be close to your mother?" There was. She sat next to my mother, and very few people were aware of her presence.

A few days later, my father's ashes, in a bronze urn, were placed in a concrete block in the ground. Before the block was sealed, my mother surrounded the urn with a dozen red roses from Mrs. Roosevelt—her tribute to him.

In Mrs. Roosevelt's newspaper column, "My Day," she spoke of him, concluding: "I always found him to be a warm and welcoming host and feel sure that all who enjoyed his hospitality will remember his gentle influence and interest in others."

Mrs. Roosevelt and my father had shared with each other the initial unhappy religious experiences of their childhood. Both, after the early deaths of their parents, had been brought up by rigidly self-righteous grandparents. According to Mrs. Roosevelt, the Halls had been "fanatical fundamentalists"; as a boy my father attended long, all-male services in a synagogue after being corralled by his grandfather, who chased him across New York tenement rooftops with a whip! Thus were they forced into a mindless adherence to inimical doctrine.

In time, the demanding love of a compassionate Savior, conveyed in the precise suasion of Elizabethan English in both the King James version of the Bible and in the Book of Common Prayer, became their mainstays. Great wrongs were undone. Mrs. Roosevelt, at her husband's side, became a faithful child of the Church. My father's devotion grew out of dutiful attendance at services at which I assisted or over which I presided, and it was to become my privilege to administer to him the gift of Holy Baptism.

Chapter 3

At Home in New York City

WHEN SHE WAS NOT AT VAL-KILL, Mrs. Roosevelt lived in New York City. Here she entertained at lunches and dinners; her guests were prominent people in the arts and public affairs or, just as likely, friends old and new. Conversation was always lively; often it turned to politics and international affairs.

⊛

ONE DAY EARLY in my friendship with Mrs. Roosevelt, Miss Corr telephoned me to say that Mrs. Roosevelt would like me to come to lunch at her New York apartment the following Wednesday, if that would be convenient. I realized at once that by canceling one of my classes I could accept, so that is what I did.

During the intervening days I anticipated the lunch with a sense of gratitude and deep pleasure. It was a rare privilege to know a completely uninhibited, original, vulnerable human being. My profound admiration for the person she had become was undisguised, even if it was not yet separated from the image of the great lady.

Mrs. R's mail was voluminous. Much of it was handled in the office of her New York apartment with the able assistance of Maureen Corr. *(Cowles Communications, Inc.)*

Irene, Mrs. Roosevelt's New York housekeeper, answered almost at once when I rang the doorbell. I introduced myself.

"Won't you come in? Mrs. Roosevelt is expecting you, Dr. Levy."

Irene was middle-aged and slight and had a sweet-toned voice with a pleasant accent. Her smile was genuine and most appealing. As she preceded me into the living room, I saw that Irene limped badly, a result of her years in the concentration camp, I surmised. How like Mrs. Roosevelt, I thought, to hire a servant to wait on her table, not for the purpose of augmenting her self-image, but to employ someone who could not easily have found such work.

There flashed through my mind the interviews I had had as an Episcopal priest with couples wanting to adopt a beautiful, physically perfect child, while the less fortunate but more needy child was passed by.

I was greeted by my ever-ebullient hostess, who introduced me to two other luncheon guests: Mrs. Joseph P. Lash and another woman, a German journalist. Mrs. Lash (or Trude, as Mrs. Roosevelt called her) was, I knew, the wife of the renowned *New York Post* columnist. She and her husband were long-time friends of the Roosevelts.

Mrs. Roosevelt seated us comfortably in a large, airy, sunlit room with a view of the cheery garden, nicely terraced and brick-walled. The furniture, drapes, and rugs were in happy colors; watercolors, photographs, and drawings gave the room interest and added warmth. Mrs. Roosevelt poured sherry for us into beautiful cut-crystal glasses; Irene placed silver dishes with an abundance of choice nuts beside our glasses. It was a luxurious moment to savor: to think that I could step from the bustling New York streets into another world, a gemlike room where time stood still and living was gracious.

This was an appropriate moment to produce from the pocket of my gray tweed sport jacket a box of chocolate marshmallow fudge that my mother had made for Mrs. Roosevelt. In presenting it to her, I said that I hoped she ate fudge.

"Indeed I eat it!" Mrs. Roosevelt beamed. "You shall see—after lunch."

There was talk of the need for educating young people for living abroad, since Americans were more and more being called upon to step into the shoes imperial powers were vacating.

The journalist then asked me if I had ever been to Germany. I told her that I had led a reconnaissance mission up to the banks of the Rhine preparatory to Field Marshal Montgomery's crossing at Wesel in 1945, and both before and after that had been survey chief of a signal corps platoon putting in telephone communications that moved the supply trains to the front.

Mrs. Roosevelt interjected: "In recognition of Dr. Levy's part in that three-man mission undertaken under artillery fire, he was awarded the Bronze Star."

Mrs. Roosevelt then asked me if I had ever seen Montgomery. I told her that I had, once, when his jeep paused alongside mine near Wesel. "I was impressed by the friendly, personal way he returned my purposely British-style salute; indeed, he leaned over and shook hands with me. He was dressed in a rough battle uniform. The only American generals I had seen rode in command cars and, tactlessly, wore immaculate dress uniforms." I added, "Even though it was the eve of a major assault, it was apparent that this was a man exulting in his great responsibilities."

Mrs. Roosevelt delighted me by saying, "I'm certain *that* kind of confidence grows out of a leader's sense of his own tested ability and, as Dean Pike says in his book *Beyond Anxiety*" (which had been one of my birthday gifts to her) "an absolute conviction that you are doing what you believe is necessary." She paused a moment in thought and added, "And you're relieved that *you* are in charge and not someone else."

I said I thought the last point was often overlooked, and reminded the company that Churchill had said in his memoirs that he had made a terrible second-in-command, but then had gloried in having the full power to act freely.

Mrs. Roosevelt led us to the attractively set table that was located near the center of the living room. It was invitingly bright, with a dazzling white embroidered tablecloth and matching napkins. There was a centerpiece of purple and red anemones in a small glass bowl. A crisp salad of bib lettuce was at the side of each plate, and Irene brought in a covered dish from which Mrs. Roosevelt served a steaming, piquantly flavored beef stew. There were hot soda biscuits and I noticed that the mustard pickles were served in a plain crystal dish engraved with the initials SDR (Sara Delano Roosevelt). Whatever the public may think, I mused, Mrs. Roosevelt doesn't need to put her mother-in-law's memory out of her mind!

Mrs. Lash asked Mrs. Roosevelt how she had found President Truman.

Mrs. Roosevelt explained to the other guest and me: "I was pleasantly surprised at how much thinking he had done and how much he had learned since his early days in the presidency. I can remember leaving his office in the White House after trying to talk to him about foreign policy and feeling like crying. I was appalled at how little he knew. My husband had had contact with Europe since he was a child and knew European history; and he absorbed from his mother's family a feeling for Asia and its problems. Mr. Truman," she told us, "knew American history, but nothing about the world. He had to rely on others, as General Eisenhower is doing today."

This led the journalist to ask Mrs. Roosevelt's opinion of President Eisenhower, who was receiving adverse comments in some parts of the press.

Mrs. Roosevelt replied slowly. "All his life has been spent in the military: an executor of top-level decisions.

He was, shall we say, very capable of carrying out orders given him by other persons." Her smile was unintentionally deprecating. She attempted to be kind, but agreed tacitly with my statement that the image he presented was not that of great intelligence. I said that the country needed a bold originator of policy, and that Eisenhower's failure was all the more tragic at a time when so many domestic problems needed his attention. He had come into office on a great wave of popular feeling and, being a Republican, had no debt to the South. Yet he did not grasp this double strength as a means by which to provide the moral and executive leadership that would bring about gradual integration for Black Americans.

Ludicrously, at the moment, President Eisenhower had brought in Robert Montgomery, the film star, to coach him in his television appearances, and the press was making sport of it. Mrs. Roosevelt said that it was perfectly all right for Mr. Montgomery to help him, but to give the help publicity was "silly." "Someone told the President it was good public relations," she added. "How often my husband had to say *no*, and he was right, and I learned to do it, too. As for being photographed doing something, the rule is yes if it is something you always do, but no if it is something you never otherwise do." I realized at once that that was why we never saw stilted, posed pictures of FDR.

Mrs. Roosevelt, who was wearing an apple green blouse, with a black skirt, two strands of medium-sized pearls, and her small diamond fleur-de-lys pin, then discussed working with men on committees. Her experience was that "men, as a whole, are vain and struggle for precedence. That makes them much more difficult to work with than women. Somehow the business at hand gets lost in the clash of egos."

Mrs. Lash asked about Haile Selassie's visit to Hyde Park, which had been announced in the newspapers.

The durable emperor of Ethiopia was coming to Hyde Park with a party of eleven that Saturday for lunch, but, as Mrs. Roosevelt told us, "the State Department has just telegraphed me to expect a party of thirty!"

"What will you do?" asked Mrs. Lash.

"Set up bridge tables on the lawn." was Mrs. Roosevelt's prompt reply.

"But what if it rains?" Mrs. Lash countered.

Mrs. Roosevelt laughed, spread her hands in a gesture of happy resignation, and said, "I won't think about that!"

Irene had served finger bowls with a miniature Staffordshire china flower in each. Dessert was the most delectable, paper-thin, flaky apple strudel I have ever eaten. As Mrs. Roosevelt passed the bowl of whipped cream, she said to all of us, proudly, "Irene makes *the* best apple strudel!" The servant beamed.

Over coffee and my mother's fudge, which Mrs. Roosevelt served ceremoniously, we got into a discussion about religion, particularly as fostered by the White House's reiteration of Norman Vincent Peale's pious platitudes about Americans praying to God in order to secure a stronger America, and other nationalistic attempts to possess the Infinite and so deflect any day of judgment. Mrs. Roosevelt, as we rose from the table, was saying, "We are too provincial. We would limit God to revealing Himself only to us, and that is arrogance on our part. If we succeeded, we would end up with a God that wouldn't be worth worshipping!"

I said that I agreed with her that we must never limit God to one kind of revelation. At the same time, I told Mrs. Roosevelt, I felt we also had to recognize that for each of us it was necessary to reach God through a particular revelation, usually, but not necessarily, the one we were born into. I added that I had been adopted and that my father had wished me to be baptised and brought up in my mother's Episcopalian faith, since he, regrettably, did not have one of his own.

Mrs. Roosevelt detained me as Mrs. Lash and the German visitor said their good-byes. Still standing, with her left hand on her hip in a characteristic pose, she began, "I agree with what you wrote me about the pervasive influence of his religion on Franklin's decisions. How do you propose to pursue the matter and make it into a book?"

I told her that I wanted to document the fact in three ways: first, to read all the speeches, public papers, and addresses; second, to examine his personal papers in the archives of the Franklin D. Roosevelt Library at Hyde Park; third, to talk to President Roosevelt's former associates and question them about their sense of the validity of this perspective which I believe he possessed.

Mrs. Roosevelt said, "I may go to Russia from July 1st to August 2nd for *Look* magazine—*if* I can get a passport. So, I'll tell you what to do. Plan to come to Hyde Park for a weekend in August and I'll have them get out the papers ahead of time."

Turning and striding toward the French windows that opened onto the terraces, she said, "I want to show you my garden." It was, like the room, another oasis of calm. It was on fire with red geraniums in full bloom, strategically placed. She was enchanted with it. "John Golden gave me these beautiful geraniums and sent his gardener over to put them in for me. *Aren't* they lovely? Such a sweet thing for him to do."

I remembered, then, seeing a photograph of the eminent theatrical producer on the spinet in the living room in Val-Kill Cottage. In the picture he was seated next to a younger Mrs. Roosevelt in a theater. The photograph was charmingly inscribed by him in white ink to "The First Lady."

"I *like* your tweed jacket," Mrs. Roosevelt said, as we walked back into the living room. "The diamond pattern is most unusual." I knew she wasn't just making small talk because this lady was incapable of that.

"Thank you," I said, complimented, "I've had it for seven years and it's a favorite of mine. The skeins of wool are dyed separately and that accounts for this irregular shading."

"I still wear one of Franklin's Scotch tweed coats. Happily, they're indestructible. He had it as a student at Harvard!"

Before leaving, I asked Mrs. Roosevelt if she would sign my copy of *Ladies of Courage*, her new book written with Lorena A. Hickok and dealing with women in American politics. She inscribed it to me "with good wishes" and then said, "Just leave it here and I'll have Miss Hickok sign it, and then get it back to you."

I ruefully admit I had not even thought of the co-author. Mrs. Roosevelt's correct way of thinking taught me an unforgettable lesson in courtesy.

On a late December afternoon I received a telephone call at the college from Maureen Corr. Mrs. Roosevelt had asked her to call me at once to say that one of her guests for a small dinner party that evening was suddenly taken ill, and would it be possible for me to help her out by coming on such short notice? It was to be at her house at eight and I was to dress informally.

I just had time to get home, shower, shave, change, and ring the 211 East 62nd Street doorbell on the minute of eight. It was a thoroughly enjoyable evening, an unexpected treat. I particularly valued the privilege of meeting Dr. Ralph Bunche, who, just five years before, had won the Nobel Peace Prize after he effected the crucial Arab-Israel armistice in 1949. A smiling, gentle man, he carried his vast erudition and long international experience lightly. A deep-rooted hope, qualified only by a trace of sadness in his experienced eyes, buttressed his strongly voiced conviction that the increasing efficacy of education would break down the destructive barriers of humanity's prejudices. I was struck at once by the eloquent fact that his own achievement was an earnest of that hope.

Later, when I was seated next to Mrs. Bunche, she told me that her husband was the grandson of a slave. At that moment, my admiration for him could not have been greater.

How perfectly the setting reflected Mrs. Roosevelt's life was something I had a moment to consider while chatting over a drink with her son Elliott Roosevelt. Nearby, a huge potted emblematic rosebush added its red color and unmistakable perfume to the scene. A table, whose base was a handsome carved wooden elephant, bespoke the regard of peoples half a world away, and the four sunlight-drenched watercolors by Louis Howe kept a loyal friend's memory incandescently present.

One of the guests remarked on the wonderful news released earlier in the year—on the tenth anniversary of FDR's death, to be exact—of the success of the Salk polio vaccine tests. Mrs. Roosevelt drew me into that conversation, saying, "Dr. Levy was present on the occasion when the French ambassador bestowed the Legion of Honor on Dr. Salk."

So graciously made the focus of interest, I told how the ceremony, a surprise for Dr. Jonas Salk, had taken place at the City College commencement, at which he was receiving an academic honor. I had delivered the invocation and was seated next to him on the platform. When he rose to receive the second honor, he turned to me and asked that I hold his handsomely boxed Legion of Honor. "So, for a moment," I told Mrs. Roosevelt's other guests, "I accidently basked in the reflected glory of the shy, dedicated scientist."

At dinner, Pakistan's United Nations representative, Ahmed Bodkari, interested me very much because he was wearing the school tie of his English University, and spoke of the enthusiasm occasioned by the announcement that Prince Philip, the Duke of Edinburgh, would be coming to Pakistan in the new year to play polo! It was an undeniable proof that the English way of life has a seducing effect on those exposed to it, regardless of their divergent backgrounds.

For me, a minor discovery with a lasting result occurred at the table that evening. Placed before us, as a first course, were oysters on the half shell, each deposited in its gilt-edged compartment on the Roosevelt-crested oyster plates.

Although I had never before tasted an oyster, and shared the prejudice of the ignorant in this matter, I knew I had an obligation manfully to fulfill. From the first of its tribe I ever tasted, I formed an immediate attachment to this luscious bivalve. No wonder Julius Caesar took the trouble to have them shipped to him in Rome all the way from Britain.

I was the last guest to leave because Mrs. Roosevelt had intriguingly told me when I arrived that she had something she wanted to give me before I left.

"Do sit down a moment, William," she said, and rushed off, returning to the room seconds later with an eight-by-ten envelope containing a photograph of herself taken on her seventieth birthday and inscribed, "With warm good wishes."

"This *is* the one you wanted, isn't it?" she queried. I told her that it was, remembering then that on the day of the City College Christian Association luncheon at which she was a guest last month, I had asked her if it would be out of turn for me to request a photograph. She had laughed delightedly and said, "Of course not! Would you like one of the Karsh portraits?" I replied that I'd rather have a copy of the informal birthday picture taken by a *New York Times* photographer as she sat working at her desk that October morning. Somehow it looked more like the Mrs. Roosevelt I know, I had told her. She had promised, then and there, to get a copy for me.

I put on my Chesterfield, reached into its pocket, and presented her with a small gift, a five-inch-square pillow stuffed with Vermont pine needles. She was enchanted.

"Do sit down *again*! I must tell you," she reminisced, "that this carries me back to the early years of my marriage when I used to collect and dry pine needles at Campobello and make them into sweet-smelling bags, *much* smaller than this one, for little Christmas gifts! I've always loved the outdoors smell of pine. I'll put this under my pillow tonight, and from now on I'll have that fresh outdoors scent right here in town! I couldn't be more tickled."

Chapter 4

At Hyde Park

*E*LEANOR ROOSEVELT MADE GOOD *on her promise to invite William Turner Levy to Val-Kill so that he could do research at the Franklin D. Roosevelt Library.*

Those fortunate enough to be invited to Val-Kill enjoyed a hospitality that was at once gracious and informal. Famous in the annals of hospitable Roosevelt informality was the hot dog and beer picnic at Hyde Park in 1939 for King George VI and Queen Elizabeth of England. Mrs. Roosevelt was much amused at the impact this informality had abroad; she told William Turner Levy an anecdote about the use of paper plates at a formal dinner in France, modeled after her own custom at Val-Kill picnics.

෫෯෧

"YOU WILL BE *SO* AMUSED, WILLIAM!" Mrs. Roosevelt laughed. "Last summer I invited a rather large number of United Nations delegates to a picnic at Val-Kill. They see so much American formality in New York that I thought it would be relaxing for them. And they did have a good time." She continued, "The other night at a rather posh diplomatic dinner here on Park Avenue, a charming French couple told me that at a recent formal dinner party at a country house not far from Versailles, they were astounded to find dinner served on paper plates! Their hostess explained, 'But, of course, *everyone* is using paper plates. It's the rage!' The hostess then smiled sweetly, knowingly, and said, 'Just like *Madame Roosevelt.*'"

⚜

Above all, Eleanor Roosevelt enjoyed seeing to the comfort of her guests and engaging them in the routines of life at Hyde Park. Over this first weekend, as William Turner Levy was enjoying her hospitality, she regaled him with stories of her neighbors the Vanderbilts, and introduced him to the director of the Roosevelt Library, Herman Kahn.

⚜

THERE HAD BEEN a terrific rain-and-wind storm the night before my departure from New York. The next morning, equipped with a suitcase of clothes and an attaché case of notebooks, pencils, and reading notes, I took a train out of Grand Central Station that got me to Poughkeepsie about eleven.

As Miss Corr had promised by telephone a few days before, William White, Mrs. Roosevelt's chauffeur, was waiting for me on the platform.

On the ten-mile drive to Hyde Park, I sat up front with William.

The sky was still ominous when we arrived at Val-Kill Cottage; many tree branches had been downed along the roads. It was a blustery, dramatic day that I found head-clearing and stimulating. Apparently Mrs. Roosevelt felt the same way. From her desk, which was at a front window, she must have seen the car arrive, for she was out to greet me with extended hand before I could get my bags out of the back seat.

"It's such a beautiful day . . . of its kind," she said enthusiastically, "that I thought we'd go to lunch in a perfectly lovely restaurant on the grounds of the Vanderbilt mansion. It's called the Vanderbilt Inn!" What a wonderful way to be greeted, I thought.

She preceded me upstairs to show me my room. It was a small, but delightful guest room with a good-sized bed covered with a white chenille bedspread, a comfortable-looking upholstered chair with a lamp and book table beside it, a dresser, a desk and chair, and two windows laced on the outside with ivy and looking down on the violently swaying branches of the trees outside.

"And here," Mrs. Roosevelt exclaimed, flinging open a door to the right, "is your bathroom. It has a shower but no tub. Is that all right?"

I assured her that I never take baths. She laughed delightedly and, stepping out into the hall, said, "Now, my room is here, next to yours, should you ever need anything, and you can get downstairs most easily by the way we came up. Take your time and unpack. I've only got a couple here as housekeepers, so guests unpack for themselves. Come downstairs as soon as you can." She consulted her wristwatch, and said merrily, "We should leave in about fifteen minutes!" With that she disappeared. The swish of her skirt around the corner was the last part of her my eye saw.

I quickly unpacked my suitcase, washed my hands and face, and then sat down at the desk for a moment to examine a beautiful, old-fashioned heavy silver-framed easel clock. Next, I saw that the pens were in an American Indian pottery bowl with the National Recovery Administration eagle drawn by the potter and inscribed: "Our President, Franklin Roosevelt, N.R.A. We Do Our Part." There were paper clips, bottles of ink, erasers, pencils—and a stack of writing paper and envelopes imprinted identically like Mrs. Roosevelt's, but without her name: *Val-Kill Cottage, Hyde Park, Dutchess County, New York*. There was a tall bronze lamp on the desk and several books, including a dictionary. Indeed, the room abounded in books—most in a wall bookcase and some on the book table.

Most impressive of the pictures in the room was a color photograph of Mrs. Roosevelt taken in the early 1930s by Edward Steichen. It captured her grace and serenity, her American "tennis court" freshness, and above all, the candor, vulnerability, and penetration of her eyes. I was seated now in the upholstered chair. On the book table next to it was a round Chinese pewter box, its cover having raised leaves and flowers mounted with carnelians and tourmalines. I lifted the cover and found it contained lavender flowers and rose leaves that scented the air with a pungent sweetness.

On the dresser I saw a candlestick (a good precaution against the sudden blackouts of electric power in the country), a simple linen scarf embroidered with the initials AER (Anna was both Mrs. Roosevelt's, and her mother's, first name), a blue silk pincushion with a variety of practical pins, and—the ultimate compliment—a small crystal vase with four perfect white roses.

Mrs. R's bedroom at Val-Kill. The pine-needle cushion on the chair is a Vermont one from William Turner Levy. *(Courtesy of the Franklin D. Roosevelt Library)*

As I left the guest room to rejoin Mrs. Roosevelt downstairs, I happened to glance through the open door of her room. There, above the fireplace, was a framed reproduction of the Frank O. Salisbury formal portrait of President Roosevelt seated at the White House desk. On the mantelpiece directly under the portrait was a beautiful squat silver vase containing a single magnificent red rose.

Downstairs, Mrs. Roosevelt introduced me to her other guests, Mr. and Mrs. Edward Elliott and Mrs. W. Forbes Morgan Jr. Mrs. Elliott's first name was also Eleanor, but Mrs. Roosevelt called her "Ellie." She was Mrs. Roosevelt's niece, a daughter of her late brother, G. Hall Roosevelt.

Edward Elliott was a wiry Englishman, whom Mrs. Roosevelt later told me had been in the Royal Air Force during World War II. Mrs. Morgan was Mrs. Roosevelt's cousin; her first name was Marie, which Mrs. Roosevelt pronounced in the French manner.

The five of us went to lunch together, the young children of both guests staying to have lunch either at Val-Kill Cottage or at the nearby home of the John Roosevelts. The two women visitors were both spirited and interesting, but the contrast between them was great. Mrs. Morgan was serious and attractive; she had a Midwestern twang and was subject to moments of abstraction. Like her aunt, Mrs. Elliott was direct and utterly unself-conscious, though a less complicated person, at least on the surface. Mr. Elliott and I talked a lot about England.

Mrs. Roosevelt drove us three miles north to the Vanderbilt mansion, which FDR had once called the most inappropriate house ever built on the Hudson (it was a larger-than-life copy of Marie Antoinette's Petit Trianon); yet, as president, he was happy to urge Congress to accept it as a house to preserve so that future generations might see the taste of a wealthy nineteenth-century business tycoon who went in for display. "Principally," Mrs. Roosevelt told me, "Franklin was anxious to preserve the grounds, which had been an arboretum for nearly two hundred years. As you will see, the examples of trees are magnificent. Franklin loved trees and couldn't bear to think of these being cut down." As we drove into the impressive estate grounds, I understood at once the value of what had been preserved.

A sizable building north of the mansion was, Mrs. Roosevelt informed me, the golf house. "This is where people changed before and after playing golf or tennis. Mrs. Vanderbilt never wanted her house in disorder or used in an informal way! As a matter of fact, Mr. Vanderbilt would often come over here to spend time in what he probably felt to be more homey surroundings!" She shook her head at the thought of having a house that was intended to impress others rather than be a comfortable haven for oneself.

The restaurant in the golf house was operated under government auspices. The food was simple but good, and, as Mrs. Roosevelt had so thoughtfully intended, it afforded us a sweeping view of the grounds and the lordly Hudson. There was still a dramatic sky, and several large tree branches strewed the lawn.

At lunch, Mrs. Roosevelt told us that the first time she visited the mansion was when she was invited with Franklin, then her fiancé, to spend a weekend. Mrs. Vanderbilt, she recalled with amusement, asked her, as soon as she had greeted her, what color her dressing gown was. "I hadn't the *slightest* idea," Mrs. Roosevelt told us, "for the maid had packed my suitcase under my grandmother's supervision! I'm sure I appeared very stupid to my hostess. 'Oh, it doesn't matter,' she told me, 'I'll give you the mauve room. You'll find a mauve dressing gown and slippers in the closet. I can't bear to think of the colors clashing!'"

I asked Mrs. Roosevelt whether it was possible to enjoy a weekend that began on that note. "Well," she replied, raising and lowering her eyebrows two or three times in her ineffably charming and characteristic manner, her eyes glinting with a naughty sense of fun, "it wasn't exactly an *exciting* way to be entertained!"

"How," I ventured to ask, "did Mrs. Vanderbilt spend her time?"

"I haven't the faintest idea," Mrs. Roosevelt replied, "but I remember her very proudly pointing out to me that she had decorated the pull chain in the toilet by tying the length of it with colored silk bows in graduated sizes!"

I was so incredulous, as this new vista was opened before me, that Mrs. Roosevelt continued: "My mother-in-law, who knew her well and called her Lulu, told me that Mrs. Vanderbilt had told her that she took a drive in her carriage every morning and afternoon. 'In the morning,' she carefully explained, 'on the way out, I recite to myself the names of all the kings and queens of France and their dates, and on the way home I recite them all backwards. In the afternoon, I recite the names of all the kings and queens of England and *their* dates on the way out, and on the way back, I recite *them* all backwards.'"

I said I hadn't known such things existed outside the imagination of Lewis Carroll. "Oh, but they decidedly *do*!" Mrs. Roosevelt said, a bit sadly, I thought. Then she commented, "So that's why Lewis Carroll's Duchess was quite right, it seems to me, when she said, 'Everything's got a moral if only you can find it.' Which reminds me of a telling incident," she continued. "The Vanderbilts used to entertain at dinner every Sunday, having roughly the same people every other week: Franklin's half-brother Rosy used to be among the regular guests. On one such occasion when all were seated at dinner in the palatial dining room, the butler brought in a cablegram on a silver salver and presented it to Mr. Vanderbilt, who, saying he didn't have his eyeglasses, asked the butler to give it to his wife to read. She opened the cable and then announced in a ringing voice, from her end of the long table: 'Mr. Vanderbilt, it's from *Buckingham Palace!*' She then proceeded to read the message aloud: 'Thank you so much for your thoughtful birthday greetings.' After a suitable pause, Mrs. Vanderbilt commented, breathlessly, 'Oh, the *dear* King!' The following week illness had deprived the Vanderbilts of an invited male guest, and as Rosy was considered to be an eligible single man (since he didn't live with his wife and one didn't invite his mistress), he was invited two weeks in a row. They went, he told us, through the *identical* routine—having forgotten, of course, that Rosy had been there the week before."

ON THE WAY BACK from the Vanderbilt Inn, Mrs. Roosevelt stopped at the Franklin D. Roosevelt Library and introduced me to its director, Mr. Herman Kahn. She then left me there, jauntily saying, "The car will be here at five o'clock, Dr. Levy, to pick you up."

Mr. Kahn was a stocky, slow-moving, warmly helpful man. His competence was instantly recognizable, as was his dedication to this fabulous storehouse of contemporary history. With a few searching questions, he discovered my needs and outlined the extent of the library's resources. I hadn't begun to realize the endless archives that were available: Roosevelt's correspondence, memorandums, papers of all sorts, were catalogued under his Groton School days, his years at Harvard, and then on into his public service as assistant secretary of the Navy, governor, and president, gaining constantly in bulk. Miss Margaret Suckley, FDR's cousin, was currently engaged in identifying and cataloging some fifty thousand still photos of Roosevelt. Mr. Kahn then took me to the research room, where I was placed under the care of the tall, shy, red-haired archivist, Mr. Raymond Corry, an extremely likeable Southerner whose knowledge of the material in the library was phenomenal. I discovered that very day that all who knew him held him in high esteem and affection.

The first afternoon Mr. Corry provided me with boxes and boxes of material relating to the President's childhood and school days. There were his school notebooks, compositions written for classes in English literature, leaflets from church services, announcements of dances, even laundry lists. As Mr. Corry explained to me, "His doting mother kept everything, even theater stubs. She had confidence from the first that he would be an important man, and history is indebted to her. Fortunately, her son developed the same habit of keeping all his papers." I could see by the afternoon's end that I had embarked on a long, but tremendously fascinating, task.

It was Mrs. Roosevelt herself who drove over to the library at closing time to pick me up. She was delighted to hear all that I enthusiastically told her about my afternoon's discoveries. "You must let me know whenever you want to work here and you will be most welcome," was her immediate reaction. I told her that I would like to work at the library both in the morning and in the afternoon of the next day, but that then I thought I would have to take time out to slowly, but steadily read through the published volumes of the *Public Papers and Addresses of Franklin D. Roosevelt* and through all the biographies. "In that case," she confided, "you certainly have your work cut out for you for the next few years!" I told her it would be fascinating for me and that I felt all the research would be lively. She agreed that her husband's life had not had many dull moments.

When we arrived at the cottage, Mrs. Roosevelt introduced me to her housekeeper, Marge Entrup, and her husband, Lester; then she left us to attend to some papers on her desk. The Entrups had been in Mrs. Roosevelt's employ for only a few months, and this was the first time they had ever been in household service. Prior to this they had owned a tavern, but had lost money; then this opportunity to pay off their debts had arisen. Lester was tall, slim, and dignified, with the sensitivity of a perfect gentleman; Marge was full of energy, fun-loving and enthusiastic.

"Mrs. Roosevelt told us," Marge reflected, "that we should not be so awestruck, that she just ran a simple household. Well! The first week we were here, she calmly announced, 'Marge, we'll need lunch on such-and-such a day this week for the emperor of Ethiopia!' I was ready to pack up and leave. My knees were shaking. What did I know about serving royalty—I hadn't even gotten used to serving Mrs. Roosevelt!"

Lester laughed his dry laugh and told me, "I said to my wife, we just do the best we can, and we don't let Mrs. Roosevelt down." I could see that they had been captivated by their employer.

After ascertaining what time cocktails would be served, I went to my room to shower, shave, and dress for dinner. The Entrups had told me that John Roosevelt, Mrs. Roosevelt's youngest son, and his wife would be coming over from their house for dinner.

John Roosevelt was a much taller man than I had anticipated: even to me, at six feet, one and a half inches, he seemed to tower. He was also youthful, playful, and friendly, with the winning Roosevelt smile. His wife, the former Anne Clark of Boston, was petite and vivacious and presented herself in a mannered, almost theatrical way, with a distinct style of her own that I found delightful. I judged it to be a perfect suit of armor for an obviously shy person.

"What will you have to drink?" Mr. Roosevelt asked me. "We'll start without Mother because she never allows us enough time!" He had apparently already taken orders from his wife and the Elliotts and Mrs. Morgan. My request for a very dry martini brought me just that. Mr. Roosevelt's drinks were strong and generous.

Mrs. John Roosevelt confided to me that her mother-in-law really didn't approve of drinking and so rarely allowed more than about twenty-five minutes for cocktails. As a result, she said, they had to drink fast, especially if they wanted a second drink! It seemed an amusing quirk that Mrs. Roosevelt had, but I suspected that it might encourage the wrong kind of drinking on the part of some of her guests.

The room in which cocktails were served was, someone told me, called "Tommy's room," for it had been the late Malvina Thompson's living room. The drinks were made in an adjoining small kitchen, which together with a bath and two bedrooms, now used as guest rooms, completed the wing of the house previously used by Miss Thompson. It also boasted a screened-in porch that was large enough for two dining tables.

In the living room, to the side of the fireplace before which we were clustered, was Mrs. Roosevelt's desk, undistinguished by any unnecessary objects. I did notice, though, a conventional triangular-shaped office nameplate, on which her name was misspelled "Elanor Roosevelt"! I suspected at once that Mrs. Roosevelt kept it because she couldn't bear to discredit the gift and offend the giver by not using it, merely because her name had accidentally been misspelled!

The fireplace was red brick, and a single ivory walrus tusk hung on each side of the mantle, which held a number of small wood, china, and glass animals and birds and several Persian copper-and-brass trays and pitchers. Flanking the fireplace were two sofas. A domed-top teakwood chest elaborately carved with a dragon, winged bird, and intertwining branches was used as a book table by the sofa that backed against Mrs. Roosevelt's desk.

The largest picture frame in the room was on the opposite wall from the fireplace; it contained a striking black-and-gold embroidered silk four-foot panel of a Balinese dancer. This was another room with many photographs: the relaxed President in a tartan frame; Mrs. Roosevelt launching a ship; Mrs. Roosevelt with Harry Truman. There was also a framed copy of the D-Day prayer, especially printed for the President as a Christmas gift. In a hutch against the wall I was facing there were china and glass plates and decanters, a pair of large carved jade fish with amethyst eyes, a perky pottery rooster, a cloisonné plate with a seated Oriental figure, and a hexagonal silver tea caddy. An ashtray nearby was engraved with a presentation to the President from the warrant officers of the USS *Houston* in 1935 "in memory of a happy Pacific cruise."

We rose as Mrs. Roosevelt bustled in to be greeted by her son with an embrace, a kiss, and the word: "Mummy!" After Mrs. John Roosevelt had greeted her, she announced to her son that she would have a Dubonnet *blonde* on the rocks. Marge brought in hors d'oeuvres on a large silver tray and linen cocktail napkins.

During cocktails Mrs. Roosevelt caught up on what all of her guests had been doing and told us about some interesting mail and telephone calls she had received.

At one point when I was talking with John Roosevelt, he told me that his father often came over from the big house with family and guests to sit here in front of Tommy's fireplace for a cocktail, finding it—as we did—a congenial room.

Miss Hickok arrived shortly after Mrs. Roosevelt had come down and, although she didn't drink because of her diabetic condition, she convivially joined us; I talked with her about a children's book Mrs. Roosevelt had told me she was writing.

Marge announced dinner to Mrs. Roosevelt, who wasted no time in telling us that we had five minutes before going into the dining room. Just a moment before, John Roosevelt had brought us fresh drinks! "Now, Mummy," he mock-pleaded, "make it ten minutes." "All right, sweetie," she chimed, "but we don't want Marge's dinner spoiled!"

The dining room, which I had previously passed through on my way into the kitchen, could now be appreciated in its own right. It was oblong in shape and wood-paneled, like the living room and Tommy's sitting room. Behind the head of the table, where Mrs. Roosevelt sat, dressed in a pastel summer dinner dress, were two windows; a circular stained glass medallion of rich color hung in each: one of Pegasus, the winged horse, and the other of a swan, both symbolic of poetry. I later learned that these veritable jewels of the glassmaker's art were executed by C. J. Connick, one of America's master craftsmen. Among his many important achievements were windows in the Cathedral of Saint John the Divine, and these medallions were presented to FDR in recognition of his chairmanship of the fund-raising campaign for the New York cathedral.

To Mrs. Roosevelt's right was a large three-tiered table, which held silver serving pieces: coffee and tea sets, tazzas, pitchers, covered vegetable dishes, tureens. To her left was a serving table used by the Entrups, and the swinging door into the kitchen.

The Victorian walnut dining table was generously wide and held several leaves; the dining room chairs were of ladder-back design, upholstered in blue brocade. The table was set with white embroidered placemats and matching napkins, gleaming china, silver, and glassware, a silver bowl of late summer flowers, and silver candlesticks. A breakfront contained rare family china and silver trays of all sizes, crested, monogrammed, and some with presentation inscriptions. On a carved oak side table two magnificent silver candelabra flanked a two-tiered metal basket filled with fresh fruit. On the wall above hung a striking embroidered silk picture of two cranes in a tree; it bore the embroidered words, "A token of our joy upon the President's reelection" and the signature "K. S. Kang, Seoul, Korea, January 1936."

On the wall to the right of Mrs. Roosevelt were two large oil paintings: one of two women at a well, the other of a woman counting a stack of coins; smaller oils on the same wall were pastoral scenes and river valley landscapes. There were also several brilliant oils of American Indian subjects by William R. Leigh and a lithograph by Julius Bloch of a young Depression-era American that reminded me of Tom Joad in *The Grapes of Wrath*. The wall to the left of Mrs. Roosevelt held a carved-wood gilt-edged mirror surrounded by twelve framed Christmas cards, one of which had been designed each year by the White House staff to present to the President and the First Lady.

The talk at the table was animated and a party atmosphere prevailed. When John carved the roast, he commented with amusement that "No one could carve like Father." Apparently, frugal FDR could serve an endless number of guests with the meat of one turkey—sliced paper thin! Mrs. Roosevelt heartily agreed.

"Franklin loved game," Mrs. Roosevelt recalled ruefully, "but it had to be really ripe. It wasn't something *I* looked forward to," she admitted with a nervous laugh, and then told us that FDR liked his game at the "turning point." I said I had enjoyed jugged hare in England until an Englishman in Oxford told me that to be properly aged the hare was hung in the cellar on an iron hook. When it fell from the hook, maggot-infested, it was ready to jug (in red wine). "Precisely," reacted Mrs. Roosevelt. "That would have suited Franklin perfectly."

Over coffee on the living room porch, Miss Hickok told us of Mrs. Roosevelt's domestic reforms when she entered the White House. "You won't believe the period the Hoovers were living in. The place was still furnished with cuspidors! They went—in a hurry! And Mrs. Roosevelt ordered modern cleaning equipment for the servants. Can you imagine attempting to clean that house with feather dusters and corn brooms!" I remarked jocularly that it was possible to believe anything about the Republicans, giving John Roosevelt a knowing wink. My sally was accepted in good humor by the one Republican member of the Roosevelt family.

For a short time after dinner, the children, who had dined at the John Roosevelts' house, trooped over to join us. There were Haven, Nina, and Sally Roosevelt; Forbes and Barbara Morgan; Stewart, Teddy, Laurence, and little Ellie Elliott. Mrs. Roosevelt, at someone's invitation, read aloud a poem about Theodore Roosevelt written during World War I by his sister Corinne Roosevelt Robinson, in which she characterized her brother as "valiant for truth."

I was forcibly reminded of Boswell's remark about Dr. Johnson: "He read so well, that everything acquired additional weight and grace from his utterance." I also felt that Mrs. Roosevelt had a taste for poetry that exhorted one to seek higher goals, as next she chose, particularly for the children, who sat about her on the floor in the living room, to which we had moved for coffee, Tennyson's stirring *Merlin and the Gleam.*

After the guests had said good night, Mrs. Roosevelt went to her desk in Tommy's room to work on her checkbook. She readily assented when I asked if I might sit up, too, and read the newspapers on the sofa that backed her desk.

A half hour or so later, Mrs. Roosevelt announced that she was retiring and suggested I should, too, for it had gotten late and we all wanted to rise early the next morning. I accompanied her into the dining room, where she took a plate, napkin, and fruit knife from those that lay ready by the fruit basket under the silken cranes. She handed me a plate, too, and said, "I always like a little fruit last thing at night. Help yourself." She took a pear and a banana and a small bunch of Concord grapes. When I took somewhat less, she picked up a beautiful red plum and said, "Oh, take this, too. It looks so good!"

I followed my hostess up the stairs; she turned out the lights as she went. When we reached the next floor, we paused. She leaned on the banister and said to me, "I have been wanting a quiet moment to tell you how much I admired your sermons on the Fourth of July and on 'Man's Dual Citizenship.' I've read them through twice, slowly and carefully, and I certainly wish more such sermons were preached. If they were," she continued, "I think more of our young people would go to church and fewer of the rest of us would nod during the sermon!"

I told her that I had been led to a vital sense of Christianity through reading William Temple, T. S. Eliot, C. S. Lewis, and Graham Greene; that among the preachers of our time, I most admired William Temple's published sermons and those of Reinhold Niebuhr, which I could go to Union Theological Seminary and hear.

Mrs. Roosevelt referred to two ideas I had tried to convey. One, we are baptized into two worlds; therefore, we are citizens of the state, but we are also—and primarily—citizens of Heaven. If one forgets the latter, then the state becomes tyrannical.

The other idea that she thought it important for America to remember is that the state exists to make possible the realization of our activities in a common life together.

Mrs. Roosevelt had braced herself comfortably by bending her left leg and placing her foot against the uprights of the banister while we talked. Now she decisively placed that foot back on the floor, stood erect, and admonished me brightly; "Now don't sit up late reading!" "I won't," I promised, and impulsively kissed her on the cheek as I said, "Good night—and thank you." She responded with a quick, heartfelt hug.

I did write a few brief letters while enjoying my fruit. I undressed, turned down the bed, and slipped between the luxurious linen sheets embroidered with the initial R. I felt duly privileged.

IN THE MORNING I was awakened early by the sound of Mrs. Roosevelt going downstairs with Duffy to let him out. Her other dog, Tamas, had recently died of old age. Almost immediately she returned to her room.

I showered, shaved, dressed, and went downstairs and out for an early-morning walk by the pond. It was chilly and only a few mosquitoes feasted on their first prey of the day. I was glad I had brought along a sweater, and I walked briskly, frightening a thrush and two gray squirrels. A steaming dampness was rising from the ground. A horse whinnied in the stable off to the left of John's house. Duffy joined me as I returned to the house.

Mrs. Roosevelt, dressed in a washable short-sleeved cotton dress, greeted me at the front door with a cheery hug as I kissed her good morning. "I hope you slept well," she queried without a doubt in her voice that I would answer affirmatively. Mrs. Roosevelt enjoyed her meals, slept soundly, and was ready for each new day, I was certain. I assured her that I never woke once and that I had got to sleep soon after we parted. "I just wrote a few short letters," I added.

Mrs. Roosevelt raised her eyebrows in her quizzical way and, with a touch of amusement in her voice, told me,

An early morning walk with the dogs to the pond was a regular occurrence in almost any kind of weather. *(Courtesy of the Franklin D. Roosevelt Library)*

"In the White House I always felt sorry for guests of one night only. They'd sit up all night and write letters on White House stationery to *everyone* they ever knew! They looked so red-eyed and pale at breakfast—but there was nothing to be done about it. I think we should have our breakfast now," she announced. "I suspect we'll be joined soon by the others, but," she added over her shoulder as she led the way to Tommy's porch, "you never know."

There was orange juice and grapefruit halves. I was delighted to see that when she had eaten as much as she could of her grapefruit, Mrs. Roosevelt picked it up and squeezed the remaining juice into her spoon. There was also honey in the comb, hot cereal, eggs, and bacon.

Mrs. Roosevelt had a toaster at her side on a small cart and offered a choice of brown or white bread each time I wanted a slice. She passed the hot toast in her fingers, a thoroughly ingratiating gesture. Breakfast was fun, too, I felt. Both brown and white sugar were offered for my cereal; Mrs. Roosevelt recommended the brown and I agreed with her preference. She cut generous slices of the combed honey, saying, "It's made on the place!" She placed them on her toast.

I asked for soft-boiled eggs, and when Marge brought them, Mrs. Roosevelt had her bring me a mother-of-pearl spoon. "I only have two of these left," she told me. "They come from Germany and I've always thought they were a good idea. You see, the yellow of the egg doesn't stick as it does to metal, and so it makes it more pleasant to eat with." There was a comfortable, practical luxury to Mrs. Roosevelt's way of life. I thought her choices admirable.

I told her of my observations on my morning walk. When I spoke of the fog, now cleared, as I could see through the window, Mrs. Roosevelt said that on days when it rose from the ground—"You see, I like to take early-morning walks, too!"—it always reminded her of walks in England when she was in school there. "As I look back," she said, "it seems to me I was *always* cold there. But, strangely enough, I can't ever recall being ill."

Then Mrs. Roosevelt asked if I ever got seasick. "Only once—in a winter Atlantic storm," I said, "but I would get sick all the time if I didn't adhere to my 'stay on deck in the fresh air' theory."

"That's my theory, too," she rejoined. Then I told her that when crossing the notoriously turbulent Irish Sea, I stretched out on a bench on deck—in the rain—and tied myself to it with my raincoat belt and slept all the way from Stranraer to Larne.

"I can go you one better," she laughed. "On *my* first trip over as a girl, I stayed in my bed the entire voyage. You see, I was traveling with my aunt, Mrs. Mortimer, and that's what she did, so I assumed that was the thing to do. I was such a silly goose," was her amusing judgment of her younger self.

Soon we were joined by the others. Mrs. Roosevelt and I alone had tea, which she poured herself, using an ornate silver strainer.

That morning and afternoon I worked in the library and accomplished a great deal because of the highly efficient help that Mr. Corry provided.

Mrs. Roosevelt, somewhat to my consternation, drove me over in the morning. Then, she told me, she was going shopping for local fruit and vegetables. She picked me up at noon and we drove to the cottage for a delicious lunch. Then she drove me back to my endless papers and files.

"William will pick you up about five," she said. "Tonight we're going out to dinner, to a place I think you'll like, right on the river. Henry Morgenthau is taking us."

AFTER I HAD DRESSED for dinner, I went downstairs to await the arrival of the Morgenthaus, who were to take

Mrs. Roosevelt and me to dinner. Mrs. Roosevelt told me
that the former secretary of the treasury had lost his wife
of many years and had recently married a French woman.
She also told me that they lived nearby in Hopewell Junc-
tion, and that he liked to be called Secretary Morgenthau.
They had invited her to dinner and when she indicated
that she would like to bring me along they were pleased to
extend the invitation. Mrs. Roosevelt's other guests were
dining with the John Roosevelts.

Henry Morgenthau Jr. was a big, gentle, bearlike man.
His wife was diminutive, birdlike, shy, and charming. At
Val-Kill, before leaving for the restaurant, Mrs. Roosevelt
asked if I would act as host in her son's absence and make
the drinks.

Mrs. Roosevelt was enchanted when her son Franklin
and his wife, Sue, dropped in and joined us for a drink.
They were not free to stay long, because they had to get to
their home in nearby Poquoque, New York, for dinner.
Like his brother John, Franklin was big, tall, friendly, and
boyish. He bore a strong resemblance to his father and had
great charm. Sue Roosevelt was petite, very attractive and
outgoing.

Norrie Point Inn, where the Morgenthaus drove us,
was about five miles north and strikingly situated on the
Hudson River in Norrie State Park, which also had a
marina. There was a full moon out and we enjoyed the way
it lit the river, which was lapping against the shore. A
small, dark island came partially between our line of sight
and the opposite shore; on that shore, high up, tiny lights
shone in widely separated houses.

It was a relaxing dinner party, with talk of the Morgenthau apple orchards, France, and family news. Mrs.

Roosevelt was delighted with her dinner, which included two favorites of hers, broiled scallops and coffee ice cream. The rest of us had decided on charcoal-broiled steak.

I told them of a wonderful childhood memory that my philosophy professor at City College, Yervant H. Krikorian, had told me. As a boy he was invited, with his father, an Armenian bishop, to spend a weekend cruising in the Mediterranean on the yacht of Secretary Morgenthau's father, who was at that time American ambassador to Turkey. Professor Krikorian retained a vivid impression of the ambassador's kindness to a boy fascinated by the workings of a yacht.

"It must be an incredible experience to be secretary of the treasury of the United States," I ventured. Mr. Morgenthau paused thoughtfully and then told me that, of course, you divorced it from your thinking about your personal finances. He was amusing about this, and then said, "Dr. Levy, you may be interested in an incident I've always remembered about President Roosevelt. It was at the time Franklin conceived a plan to help England. The plan became known as Lend-Lease. Well, Franklin thought of it one night in bed and worked it all out on memorandum sheets—it involved hundreds of millions of dollars. First thing in the morning he sent for me, and when I reached his office he enthusiastically outlined the plan and—giving me the papers with his figures on them—said, '*You* work out the details.' When I got back to my office," here Mr. Morgenthau widened his eyes in re-enacted amazement, "I happened to turn over the sheets that he had torn from a pad, and was dumbfounded to see that this man who thought and worked in billions had used a scratch pad he had conservatively kept for over twenty years! The sheets read, 'From the Desk of the Assistant Secretary of the Navy.'"

Back at Val-Kill, when it was time to retire, Mrs. Roosevelt stepped outside the living room door to call Duffy in for the night. In a loud, high-pitched voice, she repeatedly called "Here, Duffy . . . Duffy . . . Duffy . . . Here, Duffy!"—but to no avail. After five minutes of vain enticing, she locked the door and said with cheerful resignation, "Obviously, he doesn't want to come in!"

We helped ourselves to fruit, and Mrs. Roosevelt paused on the upper landing in front of an unusually framed print of a fox hunt. The wide frame was of oak, darkened with age, and the bottom had pieces of wood applied to it to make the fence over which the dogs and horsemen were about to jump in pursuit of the escaping fox. This time I leaned against the balustrade as Mrs. Roosevelt leaned comfortably with her shoulder against the wall. As we enjoyed the fruit and dried our fingers on our napkins, Mrs. Roosevelt asked me several questions about Biblical stories and their significance. She was tremendously interested in what I had to say about the great validity of the Adam and Eve myth, how Eve's sin was "to choose a better good for herself than the good which God had given her," in the British novelist Charles Williams' words.

Mrs. Roosevelt shook her head and said, "My grandmother taught me that every word in the Bible was *literally* true. She was absolutely immovable about that. So it discouraged me from asking any questions, and that was a very unhealthy situation. You weren't encouraged to think about the application of the truth of the story, and somehow it finally didn't get applied, except when a good sermon

clarified the meaning of something that was just incompre-
hensible before."

I asked Mrs. Roosevelt if she read the Bible often. "I
try to read it daily, at bedtime, even if it's only a page or
two. The trouble is that I'm usually so tired—I'm ashamed
to say it, but I sometimes fall asleep in the middle of my
prayers!" She seemed comforted when I told her this was
my problem, too, and that it was absolutely fatal for me to
close my eyes while saying them.

BREAKFAST THE NEXT MORNING was another cheery occasion. The set of California pottery dishes most used for
breakfast and lunch at Val-Kill Cottage was cheery, too,
bordered with large red apples and green leaves attached
to an encircling branch of tree. In the evenings, for dessert
plates, Mrs. Roosevelt favored French ones with amusing
cartoons. One set had its humor based on the ironic or
inappropriate name of a person or thing, *le mal nomée*;
another dealt with sailors, *dans la marine*, and in highly
idiomatic French poked fun at their foibles. The dinner
bell, rarely used because of the Entrups' perfect timing,
was a silver representation of Old Mother Hubbard, her
poor dog tucked under her arm; it had been her mother's,
Mrs. Roosevelt told me when I admired it.

"I thought of another story about Mrs. Vanderbilt that
I thought would amuse you," she began. "It seems my
mother-in-law heard that Mrs. Vanderbilt was quite ill.
She had her Black chauffeur drive her to the mansion so
that she might pay her respects and bring a few choice
flowers. She was shown upstairs into the lady's bedroom,
the chauffeur bearing the flowers. She found Mrs. Vanderbilt in her fabulous antique Spanish bed with its surround-

ing 'gate.' Candles were burning by the bed, which was funereal with black silk sheets. Sara Roosevelt exclaimed, 'Why, Lulu, I had no idea you were *this* sick!' To which Mrs. Vanderbilt replied, 'My dear, don't let the black sheets frighten you. I only have a cold, but my interior decorator thought they went well with my pearls!' But the best is yet to come!" Mrs. Roosevelt warned me, "for on the way home, the chauffeur confided, to the delight of my mother-in-law, 'Ma'am, now I know why those rich people don't have children. How could she expect poor Mr. Vanderbilt to jump over that fence?!'"

Soon after breakfast we were to drive down to New York. I was already packed and had gone into the living room to admire its pictures and objects when Mrs. Roosevelt entered. I asked her about the large Jo Davidson inaugural medal in a leather presentation case; it was lying on a table near a silver framed portrait of FDR with the presidential seal inset in colored enamel into the top center of the wide frame. "That is the original of the third inaugural medal," she explained. "Franklin gave it to me for my birthday the following year."

I asked Mrs. Roosevelt if she played the piano, a baby grand that occupied an unobtrusive place in the large room. "No," she replied, "I was given lessons as a child, but I was never good at playing. I just had no *feel* for it." I said that my experience paralleled her own.

THERE WOULD BE MANY MORE visits to Val-Kill to stay with Mrs. Roosevelt. Val-Kill Cottage was, I always thought, the most comfortable house in the world. In the living rooms, in the guest rooms, every comfortable chair had its own lamp to read by and its own side table for cup or glass. Franklin D. Roosevelt Jr. once said to me, "Isn't this wonderfully comfortable? You can just look at any room and recognize that Mummy has put it together."

Mrs. Roosevelt always selected the bed linens, towels, and washcloths herself and laid them out on the beds. Closets and drawers were made to accommodate the supply; many had been in use for years, and most were emblazoned with the initial R.

Helping carry a pile of linen for her once, I asked about her apparent pleasure in handling, arranging, and folding the sheets and pillowcases.

"I've always found it relaxing and rewarding, and I work out problems that need quiet thought while my hands and a fraction of my mind are busy with pillowcases or washcloths." As an afterthought she added, "Also, I couldn't do it until I had a house of my own! Which reminds me, when I was living with my grandmother Hall after my mother died, we spent the summer at her house at Tivoli, on the Hudson. It didn't offer a little girl much in the way of challenge. I got bored after a while. My happiest times were spent with the washerwoman. I'd beg to be allowed to iron handkerchiefs or napkins—just to be doing something useful. At this woman's farm I was sometimes permitted to pick berries and apples for jellies and jams, and I felt so useful doing that. But on occasion, out of sheer boredom, I'd slide down the cellar door. The moss would stain my panties green, and I'd be punished and told what a wicked child I was!"

Once when Mrs. Roosevelt was out of town and I arrived for a stay at the cottage before she did, she waited until the next morning and then knocked on my door.

"Bill, may I come in?" She immediately checked my bed upon entering. "Ah, just as I feared, percale sheets." She had them changed at once to the usual linen, which she was carrying in her arms. When I protested that I wasn't used to linen at home, she said, "Dear, I want you to enjoy them here."

After one Saturday together, we both had to be in New York on Sunday, but we planned to drive back to Val-Kill Monday morning for a longer stay. I remember it because, as we were leaving, Mrs. Roosevelt instructed Marge, "Don't change the linen on Bill's bed either—he's coming back with me."

Mrs. Roosevelt always dressed for dinner whether she was calling on you or having you in for dinner. Her husband is reported to have said that no one in the world looked "as well in an evening dress as Eleanor." He was right. She was regal—and radiant. I also knew that, circumstances permitting, she always took a tub before dressing for dinner. "It was something my grandmother taught me," she explained, "that especially as one got older it was essential never to become careless in such matters." On those occasions when we had adjoining rooms at the cottage and I heard the tub filling up, I knew it was time for me to dress, too.

It pleased me to present myself more formally than other guests. In winter I wore charcoal gray but had Brooks Brothers replace all the horn buttons with ones made of grosgrain—that was my invention—and in summer I had a madras jacket and a linen one, both with shawl lapels. Mrs. Roosevelt thoroughly approved of my sartorial compliment to her own personal style.

And the meals were something to look forward to! The dishes were simple and abundant (Mrs. Roosevelt always did the carving when we dined alone) and served with the freshest of seasonal fruits and vegetables. Bread, rolls, cakes, and pies were baked to perfection by Marge. In town, Irene made scrumptious apple strudel. Seafood was a favorite of Mrs. Roosevelt's, and when possible we enjoyed oysters, scallops, and soft-shelled crabs. With Marge standing by to offer advice, Mrs. Roosevelt would write out the menus for several days in advance, always allowing flexibility should Marge see some choice items in the market. Mrs. Roosevelt, who admired my appreciation of food, would often include me in the consultation. "Do help me with the menus . . . blueberries are in season, yes? . . . Do you like goulash? Good! . . . On Saturday night, as usual, we can have leftovers, a regular smorgasbord! But we'll have Marge bake—what? a coconut cake?" What fun!

Mrs. Roosevelt truly loved to dine. I remember once, upon entering the dining room in our New York apartment, she paused to admire a porcelain representation of Falstaff, a Royal Doulton piece, which didn't minimize his fat belly. "It's marvelous. But, Bill, do you think it tactful to have it right here—just before we sit down to dinner?" She never left a morsel on her plate, and I should add, she had a brilliant palate for fine Bordeaux.

In summertime at Hyde Park, Mrs. Roosevelt patronized a local farm stand. When I wasn't buried in the library, I enjoyed shopping with her. Once she said, "You select the melon, Bill, you did such a good job last time!"

The summer after her death I stopped at the stand for old time's sake. The woman who owned it recognized me at once. We shared a few appropriate words about Mrs.

Roosevelt and then she told me, dabbing at her eyes with her handkerchief, "My daughter was terribly ill and Mrs. Roosevelt sensed that something was bothering me. 'Tell me about it,' she said. I did. 'I will ask my doctor to talk with you about it. He'll be up this weekend.' She brought him here and I told him all I could, between customers, and he asked for our doctor's name and telephone number. Next thing we knew, Dr. Gurewitsch had arranged for a specialist to see her. Mrs. Roosevelt came by soon after and said that the specialist would treat my daughter. I told Mrs. Roosevelt that we didn't have the money for a specialist. She replied 'Don't worry. We'll work something out. We have to!' In a few months my daughter was all better. Dr. Gurewitsch said there was no bill because the specialist found the case an interesting one and learned a lot by taking it. I've never quite believed that story, but whatever the truth was, my daughter owes her life to Mrs. Roosevelt."

Chapter 5

First Lady
of the World

*W*HEN DWIGHT D. EISENHOWER *became president in*
1953, Eleanor Roosevelt had resigned her UN post to give him
the chance to appoint his own delegate. She was aware that, as a
prominent Democrat who had not hesitated to challenge the
president when she thought him wrong, she might have angered
him. But she also knew that she was experienced and respected,
and that UN appointments had hitherto been made on a bipar-
tisan basis—and she wanted to remain in her post. Eisenhower,
however, accepted her resignation with alacrity, for some reasons
that did not make the public record.

William Turner Levy was anxious to hear Eleanor Roose-
velt's account of what had happened. His chance came while
driving down to New York after a stay in Hyde Park.

৽৩

ON THE DRIVE DOWN, Mrs. Roosevelt shared her copy of
The New York Times with me. An article about the United
Nations caused me to ask Mrs. Roosevelt the facts about
President Eisenhower's not using her as a member of the
U.S. delegation to the General Assembly.

"It's a very simple story," she said tersely. "The General lost no time in firing me. It was one of his first acts after being elected. I told him that as all ambassadors automatically resign when a new president is elected, my resignation would have been on his desk by December 31, but he couldn't wait until he was inaugurated."

"But," I protested, "after your chairmanship of the Human Rights Commission and the adoption of the Universal Declaration of Human Rights, I can't understand why your international prestige and your unique capacity to deal strongly with the Russians wouldn't have transcended party politics."

"The president had commitments to others, I suspect," she said downheartedly. It was clear from her indefatigable work all over the country for the American Association for the United Nations—a private organization founded to stimulate interest in and support for the UN among Americans—that Mrs. Roosevelt was especially hurt because she had dedicated her energy to this work for world peace, since her husband's death had prevented him from overseeing his own creation.

Norman Rockwell, who had done a portrait of the General during the campaign, had told me Eisenhower's response to a question about the enormous change in responsibility that would be his if he were elected: "Well, I take advice. If I'm sick, I go to the doctor. If it's a political matter, I go to the politicians."

When I passed this reply on to Mrs. Roosevelt, she was appalled but not surprised. She added, "Then there *was* a personal matter. Perle Mesta, the famous Washington hostess, told him I had said something about his wife having a drinking problem. Now, I haven't the faintest idea if

Mrs. Eisenhower has a problem. I know I never spoke of it, and I'm shocked that he could believe I would gossip, especially when I and my family have suffered for so many years from maligning rumors! My own father and only brother died from drinking too much—it's not a matter I could react to other than with pain and deep sympathy. But I've been told he was infuriated by what Mrs. Mesta told him—and he's famous for his temper!"

We drove on for several miles in silence on the beautifully landscaped Taconic State Parkway. Suddenly, Mrs. Roosevelt turned to me and said emphatically, "Perhaps I should be glad the president didn't ask me to finish out my last year on the UN, for then I'd have had to embarrass him by not carrying that Human Rights Covenant to Paris. His accompanying letter was *pussyfooting!*" By her intonation I knew that the final word was one of the most damning in her vocabulary.

✤

Despite this official rebuff, Eleanor Roosevelt was determined to continue her work for the UN as a private citizen; she became the most powerful voice in the American Association for the United Nations. Meanwhile, she maintained her level of personal involvement in international affairs, circling the globe almost annually. She was particularly interested in the emerging nations of the third world, aware of their increasing importance and of their suspicion—sometimes amounting to open hostility—of the United States. Foreign dignitaries were regularly appalled by the treatment of African Americans in this country, a treatment to which African diplomats were sometimes subjected. Eleanor Roosevelt respected the aspirations of the "proud, emerging peoples" of these developing nations; she understood that the problem of one part of the world was "the problem of all."

In the early summer months of 1953, Eleanor Roosevelt had undertaken a round-the-world trip, spending six weeks in Japan and then stopping in Hong Kong, New Delhi, Istanbul, Athens, and Yugoslavia, where she wanted to observe how government functioned in a Communist country. This was the trip from which William Turner Levy welcomed her home in August, and he was eager to hear of her experiences.

༄

I was particularly interested in hearing about Tokyo's famous Imperial Hotel where she had stayed: Was it as impressive as we were led to believe?

"It is absolutely enchanting," she told me. "It was built with great ingenuity to withstand earthquake damage and the subsequent hazard of fire, and it has twice proved itself in this respect. In addition, Frank Lloyd Wright made it an imposing hotel, suitable for use by the imperial household when required. For example, there is a special Emperor's Entrance to the building. I loved the beauty of the Garden Court as well as the extraordinary "living" quality of the stone. Somehow it just doesn't seem as if dead stones were put in place! I think American visitors must be especially proud of our Mr. Wright when they see it."

Mrs. Roosevelt, I learned, had been invited to Japan under the auspices of Columbia University to speak to women's groups. Women in Japan were, for the first time, voting and participating in political life, a result of the democratic constitution we had imposed upon the Japanese government. "For the women it's a great, sometimes rather terrifying, leap from feudal status into modern responsibilities. I tried to answer some of their questions about the workings of a democracy."

When I commented that probably even women in democratic countries needed that kind of orientation, Mrs. Roosevelt agreed and then filled in the details of her visit to the emperor and empress of Japan, which had been simply reported as a fact in our newspapers.

Mrs. Roosevelt felt that being the one hundred and twenty-fourth emperor in his line had not conditioned the imperial personage to take an active stand and so lead his people. She suspected that she had talked to both the emperor and empress more bluntly than they were accustomed to, and she was struck by the remoteness of their presence. They were models of courtesy, of course, and more willing to talk than she had anticipated, "But," she concluded, "their faces have a masklike ability to conceal their emotions, if indeed they feel at all—in the sense that we do—injustices or acts of inhumanity." I concluded from all she related that Mrs. Roosevelt never presumed she had understood people because she had met and talked with them on one or a few occasions.

She also spoke about communism in Japan, especially in the schools, where the idealistic element in Marxism can have a strong appeal, as it did on many American college campuses during the Depression. In the course of our discussion she said that her respect for mere academics, as opposed to educators, was slight. "It is easy to get out of one's depth," she explained, "and perhaps especially so if you have several academic degrees to give you a false confidence in your abilities."

In Japan in spring 1953, the world's most famous traveler made new friends. *(Courtesy of the Franklin D. Roosevelt Library)*

❦

Many in the United States continued to support the claim of General Chiang Kai-shek to the leadership of all of China, but Eleanor Roosevelt, despite her sympathy for this claim, was always a political realist. She deplored leaders like Chiang Kai-shek who were unable or unwilling to accept hard truths.

※

WHEN I ASKED if she had gone to Taipei to see Mme. Chiang Kai-shek, she replied, "No, I purposely avoided a possible meeting because here is an example of extreme unreality in facing facts. The Generalissimo and Mme. Chiang really believe that they will return to power, although all of China, except their tiny island, is under Communist leadership. And, of course, the blind policy of our State Department is just as unrealistic. Chiang had his chance, as I see it, and he failed to grasp it! Because we wish the outcome had been otherwise, we make believe that all will be well, that we'll wake up and find it has all been a bad dream."

When Mrs. Roosevelt spoke in earnest of the folly of not facing situations as they were, her entire manner changed. Her voice hardened, she frowned for emphasis, and she used her hands to underscore her disenchantment with people in power who were misleading the people rather than telling the truth. "You cannot construct policy out of wishful thinking," she said, "and without a policy, we simply drift and are victimized."

※

General and Mme. Chiang Kai-shek were no strangers to Mrs. Roosevelt, who had previously entertained Mme. Chiang at the White House. The Chinese had won the admiration and sympathy of Americans when they came under brutal attack from the Japanese in the late 1930s and during World War II. But Mme. Chiang was difficult. She was something of a legend for her insistence on sleeping on her own silk sheets wherever she went.

ૹૹ

MME. CHIANG KAI-SHEK was one of the White House's most demanding guests. Her servants would strip her bed of linen and substitute silk bedding generously sprinkled with fresh rose petals. She was all charm, and nothing but charm.

One day when Mrs. Roosevelt was leaving the White House early in the morning, she found herself confronted in a corridor by a fleeing Chinese servant. After the terrified girl passed her, another rushing figure appeared around the corner. "I thought it must be a witch," Mrs. Roosevelt told me. "The face was red, the hair was flying, the expression was one of rage and violence—it was a mask of hatred. It was certainly no face I had ever seen before."

Mrs. Roosevelt was wrong. Eventually, she learned who it was, and realized that she had simply not seen *that* mask of Mme. Chiang's.

Mme. Chiang Kai-shek left her impression in other ways. One evening I picked up Mrs. Roosevelt to take her to Carnegie Hall for a concert and she was wearing an unfamiliar short white fur evening jacket. I admired it, saying I hadn't seen it before. It was made of baby llama and had gold bell-shaped buttons.

Mrs. Roosevelt told me that it was a gift from Mme. Chiang Kai-shek. "It's *very* special," she told me, "but I've never liked it particularly. However, it is warm. I wear it as a bed jacket!"

The intonation of her voice made this last sentence a very funny, and rather naughty, admission.

MRS. ROOSEVELT BROUGHT BACK other memories of this trip. There were a few personal moments she would always remember, such as "seeing the marble of the Parthenon soften in a rose-colored hue at sunset" and "watching children play a noisy game like modern football in an ancient amphitheater at Delphi. But I haven't even mentioned my visit with President Tito," she exclaimed. "I'll tell you about that next time!"

⚜

An opportunity to hear about Mrs. Roosevelt's visit with President Tito of Yugoslavia presented itself not long thereafter, as she and William Turner Levy chatted about famous world figures during a drive. Although committed to the ideal of communism, Tito had managed in the years following World War II to remove Yugoslavia from the tight embrace of the Soviet Union and maintain a considerable degree of national independence. In the course of Mrs. Roosevelt's visit, he and his wife entertained her on their vacation island Brioni (Brijuni) in the Adriatic.

⚜

THE PARTISAN LEADER, who had commanded 250,000 irregulars during the war and aided the Allied in the final dislodgment of Hitlerism, was certainly a colorful figure—and a controversial one—and a man Americans didn't know very much about. What one read in the newspapers was limited, and I depended for my few facts mostly on Churchill's accounts, as presented in the final volumes of *The Second World War*.

"I greatly enjoyed my visit with him at his retreat on the island of Brioni. He is, as I was sure he would be, a strong personality, but he is also forthright. I felt that he said exactly what he meant, and even if you didn't agree with his ideas, you felt that you had at least got close to his mind. Such frankness is not always characteristic of heads of state," Mrs. Roosevelt averred with knowledge borne of experience.

"Don't you find Yugoslavia's position as a Communist country—but as an independent Communist country that has broken from the dictates of Moscow—a very encouraging presence in the world?" I asked. "After all, their independence might be catching."

"I do. President Tito believes in the ideas of communism, but he admits there is no communism in practice anywhere in the world today, and certainly not in Russia. He also believes in his country's right to pursue its own interests, and not be used by either us or the Russians. He accepts aid from both sides and seems not to be beholden to either. I believe he is for Yugoslavia, and is therefore doing all he can to strengthen the country in the way he believes is best. He calls it socialism rather than communism, and from what I saw during the weeks I was there, I'm inclined to think that the word is correctly used. Certainly some of the profits go back to the workers rather than into the state, so that's a modification."

I asked Mrs. Roosevelt if he appeared to have the willing backing of the majority of the people.

"Yes, I'm sure he has. I asked him the same question, and he said that there were many who disapproved of having their lands taken from them and many who wanted a more hard-line communist regime, but that he depended on the good will of the majority of the people, who saw progress and understood what he was building. He's *paternalistically* realistic about the failings of human nature, which he feels is seldom as idealistic as we would like to think. I'm sure that is how he justifies his status as a dictator. He also had to admit that political arrests and political imprisonment continued. But he minimized it as a relatively small thing, which he expected finally to disappear.

"The country itself is rugged and beautiful," continued Mrs. Roosevelt. "It has an old culture that you are aware of, and it is an undeveloped country, but it is very friendly toward America, and I was received warmly everywhere by the ordinary man in the street or working peasant! And you'll be interested to know that even there I was asked about whether America was losing its freedom!"

Mrs. Roosevelt believed that our government should continue to give aid to Yugoslavia on a flexible watch-and-see basis. If we didn't, she said, then Tito would be forced to accept Russian aid exclusively, and inevitably be moved closer to that sphere of influence.

༄༅

Everywhere on her trip, Eleanor Roosevelt had been asked about McCarthyism. World leaders were concerned about the impact of his charges of disloyalty in the federal government and on the ability of the United States to continue its leadership role in the cold war era. She herself was appalled by Senator Joseph McCarthy's recklessness and his willingness to make allegations without evidence, which had poisoned the political atmosphere and damaged the reputations of innocent persons.

༄༅

IN A LETTER that Mrs. Roosevelt wrote me during the McCarthy era, she thanked me for reminding her of Patrick Henry's words: "If this be treason, make the most of it!" "I should have remembered it," she commented, "and I think it is most appropriate for use at the present time. I have used it in one of my columns, as I was sure you would not mind having it brought to people's attention."

Mrs. Roosevelt especially deplored that aspect of McCarthyism which intimidated people by threatening them with "guilt by association." "If I'm supposed to refrain from writing to persons or conversing with persons because *five years later* it is discovered that they were communists and therefore, by implication, *I* am a communist, or if I cannot agree with a correct idea because a communist may hold this idea too—why then I couldn't open my mouth! And that, of course, is the point."

What a contrast, I thought, between this American, distinguished in her own right and the descendant of distinguished Americans, and the junior senator from Wisconsin who, in newfound power, was arrogantly defining patriotism for his betters.

Mrs. Roosevelt's eyes flashed in anger as she spoke. "And it will silence persons less secure than ourselves," she lamented. "The atmosphere becomes poisonous when people speak guardedly because they distrust each other. You have blacklists, and jobs jeopardized by informers."

We lamented, as well, the effect repression at home was having on our allies abroad, who depended on the presence of an unfalteringly democratic, if not serene, America. I told Mrs. Roosevelt that I felt sad having to "explain" McCarthyism to European friends.

I was deeply troubled and must have showed it. Mrs. Roosevelt cheered me. "We just have to keep on speaking out," she said. "Time will show an increasing number of people that no one is safe under these circumstances—not even themselves—because the tests of loyalty keep changing, as they did during the Reign of Terror in France."

Mrs. Roosevelt's common sense and long perspective impressed me. She had been born in 1884 when Victoria was still on the throne in England. I realized that here was a woman who was born when transportation meant the horse-drawn carriage. She had seen the arrival of the electric light and the radio, and the whole order of society had changed in her lifetime.

As though she had been reading my thoughts, she startled me by saying, "It's difficult for anyone as young as you to realize that this has all happened before. Progress, as we believe in it, has always had temporary setbacks." Then she reminisced, "Just think, though, how far we have come. I was the first Roosevelt woman to work, to take a job—teaching. I remember that it horrified Franklin's mother even more than it fascinated him! Franklin had never been in a slum until he picked me up once in downtown New York, where I was doing social work."

"And," I said, smiling incredulously, "you saw Queen Victoria's casket borne through the streets of London." She followed my train of thought. "It was hard to believe that she could die. She had been queen of England for more than sixty years! I can still remember how surprised I was when that coffin came into view. Nothing had prepared me for the sight of anything so tiny! To think that these were the remains of a woman who would give her name to an age."

Chapter 6

The World Comes to Call

VAL-KILL WAS Eleanor Roosevelt's preferred site for entertaining the world leaders who regularly called to pay their respects when they were in the United States. Four of these visitors, each memorable in his own way, were the shah of Iran, Soviet leader Nikita Khrushchev, President Tito of Yugoslavia, and Emperor Haile Selassie of Ethiopia. While the shah was an ally of the United States during these years of the Cold War, Nikita Khrushchev represented the repressive Soviet Union, and President Tito, though a rebel from Stalinism, still professed allegiance to the Communist system.

William Turner Levy, invited by the rector of Saint James's Church in Hyde Park to preach a guest sermon, took the occasion of Khrushchev's visit to remind his listeners that the United States was not blameless in its confrontation with the Soviet Union. This country needed to witness to a conviction of the essential unity of all human beings "by ourselves overthrowing the wall of partition which divides one American from another today."

When President Tito visited Val-Kill, on the other hand, Levy challenged him about academic freedom in Yugoslavia. Mrs. Roosevelt assured him that he was not out of order to press Tito on this issue: "He will remember the honesty of your doubts about his system."

�❧�

MRS. ROOSEVELT WAS HOST at Hyde Park to Mohammed Riza Pahlavi, shah of Iran, who had succeeded to the Peacock Throne upon the abdication of his father in 1941. He was heir to the ancient Persian Empire largely created by Cyrus the Great in the sixth century B.C., with a population of forty million subjects, the greatest empire the world had ever seen.

Mrs. Roosevelt admired his progressive tendencies, knowing that he felt his country's salvation lay in making land reform a reality. He was also internationally minded, with strong ties to the United States and a desire to make Iran's support of the United Nations a fact.

She told me, however, that when she escorted the shah into the President's office at the Franklin D. Roosevelt Library to show him the priceless rug he had presented to her husband, he shocked her.

Kneeling down, he raised a corner of the rug to explain that the incredible number of knots per square inch was the measure of the rug's great value. It was a royal treasure! "Only the tiny hands of the youngest children are capable of tying them," he proudly announced to Mrs. Roosevelt's utter dismay.

"I trust I covered my reaction well," she told me, "for it had been a regal gift and well-intended. Clearly, he was not yet progressive in regard to child labor."

In 1959, the shah invited Mrs. Roosevelt to Teheran. "One is hardly prepared for the opulence," she reported upon her return. "The crown is comprised of more than ten thousand carats in gemstones, and the Peacock Throne is covered with more than twenty-five thousand jewels of magnificent color and beauty. If I understand correctly, these extravagant jewels back up a large part of the country's currency. But I was captivated by the Persian miniatures in the Imperial Library: battle scenes, royal portraits, hunting scenes, garden pavilions—and remarkable examples of calligraphy with fabulous floral backgrounds, all brilliant in color and delicate in execution. And, William, the monumental ruins at Persepolis seen at sunset spoke volumes about the transitory nature of the greatest worldly power."

Twenty years later the revolution of the Ayatollah Khomeini brought the shah's reign to an end. Power is indeed transitory. I think of this each time I polish the intricately hand-wrought silver nut dishes Mrs. Roosevelt found for me in Teheran. In each is embedded a silver coin with the likeness of one of the shah's royal progenitors.

As Shelley quoted the imperial tyrant Ozymandias, "Look on my works, ye Mighty, and despair!"

NIKITA S. KHRUSHCHEV, the premier of Soviet Russia, was coming to Hyde Park! Well, he was coming to tour the United States as a guest of President Eisenhower. It was 1959, two years after Mrs. Roosevelt's almost month-long trip to Russia and her stormy interview with Mr. Khrushchev. Preparations for Mr. Khrushchev's visit were hectic, and had their humorous aspects, as was the visit itself.

"Security," the safety of the visitor, was paramount in the minds of all the responsible American officials. Two rather unimaginative young men in black suits arrived at Hyde Park to make all necessary "arrangements." They felt that when Khrushchev visited the Franklin D. Roosevelt Library, it was absolutely imperative that he enter and leave by the *exit* to the building, which alone could be perfectly protected. However, upon consulting their Russian counterparts they were flatly told that Mr. Khrushchev could not possibly "sneak" in through a rear door. Stalemate. One of the young men told Mrs. Roosevelt that they were at their wits' end, and no solution seemed possible. I saw Mrs. Roosevelt smile innocently. She had a suggestion to offer. They were all ears. She said, "Have a sign made that reads 'Main Entrance' and place it on the exit door." The problem was solved.

Mr. Khrushchev's final stop after the gravesite and library would be at Val-Kill Cottage for a light repast. His time was very limited. In effect, he was being whisked up the parkways from New York and then back down to the city. The parkways were closed to all traffic during those hours and policemen were stationed on every roadway bridge that crossed them.

Then Mrs. Roosevelt was told by the security team: "One final point is that we have decided it will be necessary for security reasons to cut down the trees around Val-Kill Cottage."

It didn't take Mrs. Roosevelt a split second to react: "Absolutely not! I will not have it! If the Secret Service was able to protect my husband when he visited here as President, they can certainly protect Mr. Khrushchev. I don't care if you have to put a man behind every tree!"

The Sunday before the Khrushchev visit to Hyde Park, which was not Mrs. Roosevelt's idea, but originated at the request of the State Department, I was invited by the rector of Saint James's Church in Hyde Park, at the suggestion of Mrs. Roosevelt, to preach the sermon. I was both honored and at the same time determined to use the "bully pulpit," as Theodore Roosevelt would have said, to confront the parishioners with the danger of shifting the evil in the world onto the shoulders of our adversaries, the Communists, without recognizing that our own less than splendid example was partly responsible for fueling their success.

After the service, I drove back to Val-Kill Cottage with Mrs. Roosevelt for Sunday dinner. She took my arm as we walked to the car, squeezed it warmly and gave me a smile radiant with approval. Being the aristocrat she was, she said nothing, well-aware that I knew I had fulfilled my mission with honor. Later in the week, her secretary, Miss Corr, telephoned to say that Mrs. Roosevelt would like two copies of the sermon, one for the files of the Franklin D. Roosevelt Library and one for herself.

A few days after the Khrushchev visit, Mrs. Roosevelt telephoned to regale me with two anecdotes:

"You will love to hear that I had the director of the library move the glass case containing the Roosevelt family Bible, on which Franklin took the oath of office as President four times, to the new 'Main Entrance' so that Mr. Khrushchev could not miss seeing it no matter how limited his time. Even so, he would have walked past it if I had not paused to point out that on each inaugural occasion the Bible was open to First Corinthians, chapter thirteen, on which Franklin placed his hand. I then read it aloud to him, whether he liked it or not: 'Though I speak with the tongues of men and angels, and have not charity, I am become as sounding brass, or a tinkling cymbal.'

"Oh, he really had no time at all at the cottage, so you missed nothing by not being able to be here. It was a whirlwind stop—not even time for a bite! As he passed the table on his way out, he grabbed a roll, held it aloft for the reporters to see, and grinning broadly, said, 'One for the road!' You can just picture Marge. She said to me afterward with a dazed look on her face, 'Just think—*my* roll!' "

Mrs. Roosevelt would have another chance to see Mr. Khrushchev the next year, when he came to this country to scold and threaten the UN General Assembly and the Western democracies in what could only be termed a display of outrageous bad manners. He accepted her invitation to tea at her New York town house. She told me, confidentially, that for all his public bluster and bravado, he confessed to her his fear of the Chinese. "He was terrified by their immense population, saying, 'They could bury us, suffer equal losses, and survive!' "

Mrs. Roosevelt invited me to Hyde Park in the spring of 1960 to meet her guest Vladimir Dedijer, a Yugoslav delegate to the United Nations and a strong supporter of human rights everywhere in the world. She told me that he had been a partisan comrade of President Tito's and that they had fought side by side against the German and Italian occupation forces during World War II. He had also written a biography of Tito that had been translated into more than thirty languages because of its importance in explaining the evolution of Yugoslavia's independent style of communism. Yugoslavia's independence resulted in Stalin expelling the nation from the Soviet bloc.

Dedijer was a big bear of a man, immensely warm-hearted and likeable. I found him to be a remarkable figure, strong but playful and boyish, possessed of a subtle mind and obvious leadership qualities; there was also a tragic cast to this man, who had seen and done heroically demanding deeds.

His frankness was refreshing. "I'm a peasant of the Danube," he said. "What I think comes out! And, no, that is not good. Oh, to be like the British, controlled." He added, shrugging, "I'm sensitive, love gossip—well, I was brought up in a girls' boarding school!"

Before breakfast the next morning, returning from a walk, he announced, "I talked to a bird this morning. He told me that I don't write enough." He paused reflectively, explaining, "Always, as partisans, in the morning a bird would be with us, having followed." It was a sentence so simple, so unexpected, so nostalgic, that for an instant you were transported to a past not your own.

"Tito was like a father to us," he told Mrs. Roosevelt and me. "He took care of us. He presided over our meals, carved, passed our plates, served himself last. When my wife was killed at my side, it was Tito who dug her grave with me." The intensity of his personal affection was profound. "I believe in great leaders. Tito is essential to Yugoslavia's survival as a nation."

Yet this was the man who backed Milovan Djilas when he was deposed by Tito for his independence. Djilas was imprisoned, and Dedijer was put under house arrest for six months, a kind of suspended prison sentence. He remained a dissident, this former political commissar with the rank of lieutenant colonel.

"Conviction is required in a man," he continued. "Of course, once believed, the ideology becomes all. Look at de Gaulle. You in America believe in self-determination. That is your strength. You must have ideas to lead. You must never be complacent, never let down your guard militarily. Your films show the world a land of plenty, good—but there is envy out there. I have suffered for defending America." He thought for a moment, then. "You could have trouble in the future—the haves and the have-nots."

At one point Dedijer and Mrs. Roosevelt were discussing Castro. He said, "I know how he feels. I've been through the same thing. You feel a surge within you—that nothing is impossible!"

Mrs. Roosevelt remarked, "I feel that we should have given him the loan, helped him when he needed it and was alone—with the strict proviso that he accept either from the UN or from us advice on establishing a government and stabilizing it. I have the feeling that he is a revolutionary leader but that he is not able to rule. But my idea of having him beholden to us fell on deaf ears in the State Department."

At once a great patriot and a staunch internationalist, Vlado, as Mrs. Roosevelt told me his friends called him, was wholesome, independent, beholden to none. His sense of humor was delightfully original. At breakfast, Mrs. Roosevelt offered him hominy. "In the South they take it with butter, but in the North with brown sugar and cream." "I'll take both," he replied. "This is an issue I do not want to take sides in."

NOT LONG AFTER, when President Tito visited the United States to address the UN General Assembly, he asked our State Department to arrange for him to visit Mrs. Roosevelt at Hyde Park. He wished to honor the memory of President Roosevelt and to spend some time with Mrs. Roosevelt, whom he had entertained at his island retreat on Brioni in the Adriatic.

As was usual when none of her sons were present, Mrs. Roosevelt had asked me to serve drinks to her guest. With both American and Yugoslav Secret Service men guarding President Tito, I thought to myself, "He better not choke on the drink, or worse yet, keel over!"

Having been introduced, I asked, "Mr. President, what would you care to drink?"

"Cognac?" he queried.

"Yes, sir. Remy-Martin?"

He smiled broadly. "Excellent!"

I ostentatiously brought an unopened bottle to his side table along with an appropriate glass, leaving the already opened bottle in the cabinet. I then proceeded to open the bottle in front of him and poured as he held the glass. I then left the bottle on the small tray. Looking back on my maneuver it seems rather far-fetched, but at the time I was certainly intimidated by so much security in the room.

Tito was heavyset, wore a rather too beautifully tailored dark suit, a white shirt, a red tie, and a white pocket handkerchief. Although his hair was graying slightly, his tanned face was without wrinkles. His presence was that of a head of state, but his demeanor was unassertive, even modest. His gold wristwatch had an intricately worked gold band. He wore a diamond ring on the fourth finger of his left hand and a diamond tie clip. He smoked Robert Burns cigars in an ivory-and-gold holder.

With the aid of an interpreter he spoke of his un-bounded admiration for President Roosevelt and how shocked he had been by his premature death. "Not to ful-fill his work after the great effort with which he carried out the war!"

When asked if he felt that seven years in jail had been formative for him, as polio had been for FDR, he unself-consciously bent over and retied a shoelace, answering, "Yes. It gave me time to study. But that was after two years in solitary confinement. The new head of the prison was a comrade in the same regiment in World War I, and so I had books."

Representatives of the major news agencies were pres-ent; however, Tito made it clear that this was not a press conference but a private visit. At one point when the pho-tographers shouted, "One more!" he mildly reprimanded them, "One, and then one, and then one more!" It was good-natured.

At one point he turned to talk to Dr. Gurewitsch and myself. I told him that I had met Vladimir Dedijer and liked him very much. He was dismissive. "Oh, Dedijer, Dedijer!" He frowned. I spoke earnestly when I repeated what he told me of the partisan years and how he consid-ered Tito the father of his country. President Tito thrust his hands into his jacket pockets and seemed very content.

Tito knew I was a teacher, and he asked me where I taught. (In fact, he knew a number of things about me. Later, Mrs. Roosevelt explained that a guest list is always submitted to a head of state. I was glad I passed his scru-tiny because I found out that another guest had been

At Val-Kill, with Dr. Gurewitsch and President Tito of Yugoslavia on the occasion of our discussion of academic freedom in his country. *(Courtesy of William Turner Levy)*

rejected.) I told him that when my students heard that I was to have the privilege of meeting him, they wanted me to ask about academic freedom in Yugoslavia.

"Academic freedom? Yes, yes, we have academic freedom," was his answer.

"In all subjects?" I pursued. "In every way?"

"Too much, sometimes," he retorted, slightly raising his voice. "Too much freedom for the professors."

"But the students?" I said. "Are they free to discuss your political opponents?"

"I do not understand," he replied, with more agitation. "Djilas, Djilas," he all but shouted. "No, no, they would not mix in such things! Never!"

"But, sir," I wished to continue, "then you do not have academic freedom in the sense that we do."

He reddened under his tan, turned abruptly, and strode away.

I kept away from him for the meal and the rest of the visit. All attention had been on us, and he was displeased. Later, the press representatives crowded around to congratulate me, saying, "We could never do that. You can't talk to a head of state like that. You were wonderful, you were free to do it and you did. Good for you—he won't forget you."

When I sensed that preparations were being made for the president's departure, I retreated into a small room off the beaten path. Suddenly, I was aware of a hush in the house. The next thing I knew, Tito, alone, came to find me. He was formal but correct.

"I want to say good-bye," and he offered me his hand. We were alone; no one followed him. He smiled genuinely and I did, too.

"I must say, Mr. President, that you disappointed me."

His face fell.

I quickly added, "It is well known that you are married to one of the most beautiful women in the world—and you do not bring her."

Mrs. R with President Tito at Hyde Park. *(Courtesy of William Turner Levy)*

He beamed. He took my hand in both of his. "I will bring her next time. You are very kind." He turned with a kind of valediction and was gone.

That evening when the rest of the household had departed or retired, I approached Mrs. Roosevelt rather sheepishly. She said, "Wasn't that extraordinary of him? He missed you at the door."

I told her of my astonishment and the happy ending.

"You would make a good diplomat," was her smiling comment.

"But I didn't know he could speak English."

"Of course, he can, but the use of an interpreter gives him time to frame his answers. Clever?" She winked. I knew she was not upset with me. But I did ask her if I had done wrong.

"Really, Bill! I invited you because I wanted him to meet you—not just to have you meet him. He is, as you can see, a very intelligent man—and he will remember the honesty of your doubts about his system."

I decided that Christmas to send a Christmas card to President Tito. It was an impulse to return his graciousness to me. At New Year's he sent me a card. I couldn't wait to show it to Mrs. Roosevelt.

"Just look," she crowed. "He signed it Josip Broz."

ON ONE OF OUR DRIVES to the library, I asked Mrs. Roosevelt about the visit she had had from Haile Selassie. She told me that she was impressed with his keen interest in how the records of Franklin's administration had been preserved and catalogued at the library. It was something she felt he would put into practice in Addis Ababa when he returned home. "But what was most amusing," she concluded, "was that our State Department insisted I provide the emperor with a room in which he could meditate and pray, for a full half hour. Well, before lunch His Majesty was watching television—a novelty for him—when I suggested he might now like to have his 'quiet time.' Not a bit of it! He told me that he only wanted the privacy to take off his shoes in case his feet hurt, as he was unaccustomed to Western shoes, but—and here he pointed down to his stocking feet—'You see, my shoes *are* off!' Visiting Val-Kill Cottage, I'm happy to say, was obviously a more comfortable experience than he had been able to anticipate."

Later, Mrs. Roosevelt showed me the gift sent by Emperor Haile Selassie. In a bedroom off Tommy's living room she turned on the lamps in the room, and I saw a large oriental rug with a subtle, small-scale design of many colors on a burgundy background. It had an inscription woven into one edge.

"Since we spoke of his visit I wanted you to see this, and . . ." she paused, raising her eyebrows in delight, "he also sent four hundred pounds of Ethiopian coffee—in beans! I hope you will like Ethiopian coffee!"

We agreed that the emperor did things on a royal scale.

Chapter 7

A Fondness
for Young People

WORLD LEADERS WERE NOT the only ones to be fêted at Val-Kill. Eleanor Roosevelt had a particular fondness for young people, which was most definitely reciprocated. She gave an annual picnic of hot dogs, potato salad, cole slaw, fruit, and ice cream for the students of the Wiltwyck School, a school for troubled boys that she had long supported. A highlight of the occasion was her reading from Kipling's Just-So Stories.

Eleanor Roosevelt also enjoyed being with college students. William Turner Levy, who taught at the Bernard M. Baruch School of Business and Public Administration of the City University of New York, would from time to time take his students to Val-Kill to meet her, and on several occasions she spoke at the college.

༄༅

"MRS. ROOSEVELT! . . . Mrs. Roosevelt! . . . Mrs. Roosevelt!" a swelling chorus of boyish voices, enthusiastic, even possessive, emanated from scores of running youngsters dashing across the lawn at Hyde Park toward the picnic area. It was the start of the annual Wiltwyck School outing that we had all anticipated.

There was work for all hands: tables had been set up, bowls of salad and fruit had been carried out, fires were lit, an incredible number of frankfurters were piled high and waiting to be grilled, tubs of ice cream, still covered and icy cold, were ready to be dished out.

Mrs. Roosevelt was surrounded. Each of the guests had to greet her, and the "old boys" introduced the boys "new" to the party this year.

The buses were now empty and the counselors and teachers were joining us. Wiltwyck School, located nearby, was a nonsectarian, interracial, and nonpunitive institution for "neglected and delinquent" boys between the ages of eight and twelve. Most of them knew Mrs. Roosevelt well and recognized her as a friend, for she visited them during the year and on such occasions read to them and talked about her travels to places as far off as Thailand and India.

The picnic had become a ritual over the years. All of us were caught up in the excitement and eager to help; sisters-in-law, if present, cousins and grandchildren old enough to help, foreign visitors—all took up positions.

Uncle David Gray, in his eighties, wearing one of his usual magnificent butterfly bow ties unerringly poised on the center of his shirt collar, would hand out the large paper napkins. Then willing volunteers would serve the potato salad, the cole slaw, the frankfurter rolls conveniently split. A ritual indeed.

Mrs. Roosevelt told me that once she decided to serve macaroni salad as a change from the ubiquitous potato salad. "It was a terrible mistake. The 'new boys' had been told just what to expect, so anticipation was high, taste

Each year Mrs. R invited students from the Wiltwyck School
for "neglected and delinquent" boys to a picnic at Hyde Park.
Most of them knew her well and recognized her as a friend.
(Courtesy of the Franklin D. Roosevelt Library)

buds prepared, and then—disappointment." She shook her
head ruefully. "Well, I never made that mistake again."

What fun we all had! The youthful enthusiasm was
contagious. As we who were the "help" carried the empty
serving dishes away and tried to find room to stack them
somewhere in the kitchen, Mrs. Roosevelt started up the
games, which included jumping contests and races of all
kinds. Out came the buckets of wrapped candies, the prizes
for each performance.

Each boy took his turn and Mrs. Roosevelt, a close observer, awarded the always-equal prizes to one and all.

I knew from the past what was going on. It was Mrs. Roosevelt's annual physical checkup of the boys. "I particularly watch the vigor of the jumping," she had told me. "That way I can check them for rickets." I knew that she also worked at increasing their attention spans. "It's very simple," she confided. "Each time I read Kipling to them—and it's always the *Just-So Stories*, that's what they expect, just like the potato salad—I make the reading longer. It works like a charm!"

The eager group surrounded Mrs. Roosevelt's chair when she brought out the book. Not a sound was heard, eyes were all on Mrs. Roosevelt, and the spell was cast. Perfect stories perfectly told with changing voice tones to suit the characters. What a delight it was for all of us. This year it was "The Elephant's Child," followed by "Rikki-Tikki-Tavi."

And so they heard from Mrs. Roosevelt how the elephant got his trunk. She obviously loved the Elephant's Child for his "satiable curtiosity." She spoke his lines in a tiny, child's eager voice; the voice of the Kolokolo Bird was mournful; the voice of the Crocodile of the Limpopo River was filled with cunning, and, when he grasped the nose of the Elephant's Child (for he as yet had no trunk) in his jaws and spoke between his clenched teeth, his voice became cold and cruel. The comedian of the piece, the Bi-Coloured-Python-Rock-Snake, was rendered marvelously funny by her quirky intonations.

Still echoing in my mind, as well, were the opening lines of the poem that comes at the end of the tale, and that she had just recited so tellingly:

I keep six honest serving men;
   (They taught me all I knew);
Their names are What and Why and When
   And How and Where and Who.

I saw that the children loved the sound of the story and that Mrs. Roosevelt's eloquent hands wove the meaning permanently into each consciousness.

Then the older boys brought out huge empty oil drums from a station wagon. The drums were painted in geometric designs of brilliant color. They played and sang the most exuberant and haunting calypso songs. How strange it was to hear this West Indian sound as we sat on a lawn in the Hudson River valley. It may have been the first time ever. It was their proud gift to their friend.

Soon they would be off, the day would end, but not the memory of it, not for any of us.

A few of the boys went up to the house to use the "facilities." I took the opportunity to return the book to its wonted shelf in the library. Two boys were several feet in front of me as we were leaving the house. One of them reached into his pocket and showed something to his friend. The friend asked, "Where'd you get that?" I did not hear the answer. The friend grabbed him roughly by the shoulder, pointed back to the house, gave him a shove, and said in an indignant voice, "We don't steal from *Mrs. Roosevelt!*"

I trailed along as Mrs. Roosevelt accompanied her guests to the buses. Several, in turn, hung on to her hands, looking up with smiles and exclamations of thanks. One said, "Mrs. Roosevelt, I'm Johnny." "Of course, you are," she replied smiling broadly.

One shy boy of about ten sought a private moment with the wonderful lady. "Mrs. Roosevelt, do you remember me?"

"Of course, you silly goose. How's your sister?"

MRS. ROOSEVELT WAS a good friend of the Bernard M. Baruch School of Business and Public Administration, a college of the City University of New York, where I taught and which was named for the distinguished alumnus and her friend.

Louis Sherry's much admired fine chocolates sold in lavender tin boxes decorated with violets were sometimes Mr. Baruch's choice of a gift for Mrs. Roosevelt and her guests, and we marveled that they could be obtained in a gigantic ten-pound box. The generosity was admirable.

Mr. Baruch was a colorful figure, and my students told me that he unexpectedly squired Mrs. Roosevelt to a senior prom one year. The students were overwhelmed by the honor. A waltz was struck up and the elegant couple took to the floor. Gradually, the students left the ballroom floor to them, circling it, enthralled by their grace and flair and high enjoyment of an art they had possessed for half a century. The music over, Mr. Baruch bowed deeply and kissed her hand; she curtsied, and as he escorted Mrs. Roosevelt, resplendent in a pink silk evening gown, to their table, the room broke out in thunderous applause. One of my students said that he felt they had glimpsed the heady romanticism created by Strauss waltzes in "old Vienna."

AFTER HER FIRST VISIT to Russia, an event of great interest to the news media, Mrs. Roosevelt consented to address the entire student body and then to entertain their questions. It was a day of great excitement on campus. On another occasion the school held a symposium on "FDR: The Man and the Statesman," which Mrs. Roosevelt consented to be a part of.

I suppose that young persons were first attracted to Mrs. Roosevelt because she was a household name, the widow of a great president, and one who linked, for them, the heroic past to the present in which they lived. They caught from their elders the sense of awe in which she deserved to be held, for there was something almost legendary in the very quality of her life.

Yet when college students did meet her—and I often took groups of them up to her cottage at Hyde Park for "press conferences"—it was not at all as they had expected it would be. Her utter simplicity, candor, and interest in them engendered their own responses of admiration and affection: they had no need to lean on the stories their parents had told them about her.

In the Depression and in war she had undoubtedly been a great strength to her husband and to the American people, but they were now in direct contact with her greatness and for them it was to be found first of all in her desire to help them. Out of her wise assessments of the past and her shrewd understanding of the present, she helped them to think out their problems and the world's in realistic, yet generous terms.

There were no easy answers, but there were answers—provided one accepted honestly each challenge and worked tirelessly for a just solution. Sitting on benches or logs or the corners of the children's sandbox by the stream behind the cottage, the new generation learned not only the living validity of the past, but the way in which it could help shape the present and the future.

At a picnic lunch for my students at Val-Kill Cottage, Mrs. R
and I watch as they open their gift to her of Australian candied
apricots. *(Courtesy of William Turner Levy)*

Mrs. Roosevelt taught them to look ahead with confidence in order to succeed, as Americans before them had
always succeeded. Her lessons reflected the boldness of her
mind, and the youthful "gaiety" that Yeats has called the
quality of the profound.

They would always bring a gift that they would first
check out with me for appropriateness. My usual sugges-

tion was a box of Australian candied apricots—a favorite which she always insisted upon sharing with them.

After Mrs. Roosevelt's report on her Russian trip, to spare her a lunch with college officials, my mother and I arranged to take her to lunch ourselves and ordered a taxi to be at the college entrance.

Word about Mrs. Roosevelt's appearance was out in the neighborhood. When we left, both sides of 23rd Street and Lexington Avenue were jammed with people hoping to see her. Police had arrived. Traffic was at a standstill. We inched our way to the taxi and then the driver inched his way into the street. The police finally cleared a path through the cheering, waving crowd. Faces pressed against the windows were all we could see of the street. Mrs. Roosevelt was gracious to the crowd, but not encouraging.

I was somewhat emotionally exhausted, and we were twenty minutes late at the restaurant, a favorite French one of ours.

When the traffic flow finally returned to normal, I turned to Mrs. Roosevelt sitting in the back seat and remarked that although the universal applause was not for me, I was enormously stimulated by so exhilarating an experience.

Mrs. Roosevelt, turning to my mother, smiled, and said, "Just like my husband."

Chapter 8

Celebrations . . .
and Memories

READING ALOUD at picnics and special occasions, and above all in the evening after dinner, was a cherished tradition of Eleanor Roosevelt's. One of the few entertainments available to families in the Victorian era in which she had grown up, it remained a beloved ritual that was especially memorable around the fireplace in the dark of winter.

ॐ

WHAT A SPECIAL ENTERTAINMENT it was when upon occasion, after dinner at Val-Kill Cottage, Mrs. Roosevelt could be induced to read aloud. More usually it would be in late fall or winter. We'd gather by the great stone fireplace, our attentive faces lighted by the flames, and the periodic explosive crack of the wood added its seeming participation.

Favorite passages would be repeated over the years as though we could not have enough of them, an ever fresh nourishment. From *John Brown's Body* by Stephen Vincent

Benet, Mrs. Roosevelt would choose the opening, the closing, the dance, and the mistress of the plantation:

> She was often mistaken, not often blind,
> And she knew the whole duty of womankind.
> To hate the sin but love the sinner
> And see that the gentlemen got their dinner.
> And never, never to lose the charm
> That make the gentlemen offer their arm.

There were passages from Tagore's books, and from Gibran's *The Prophet* passages on love, marriage, children, and rich men.

She introduced us to Countee Cullen's poems, including one on Sacco and Vanzetti and the opening of "The Black Christ."

No one could ever forget or be the same after hearing Mrs. Roosevelt read Corinne Roosevelt Robinson's poem about her sister, so crippled by arthritis that all movement was denied her. Each morning she was dressed and lifted into a chair until she was again lifted and put to bed at night. Though almost deaf, this aunt of Mrs. Roosevelt, Theodore Roosevelt's sister, was one she and other young members of the family turned to for a sympathetic ear and wise advice. The poem was written during World War I and entitled "Soldier of Pain":

> Not in the trenches, torn by shot and shelling,
>   Not on the plain,
> Bombed by the foe; but calm and unrebelling,
>   Soldier of Pain!
>
> Facing each day, head high with gallant laughter,
>   Anguish supreme;
> What accolade in what divine hereafter
>   Shall this redeem?

Through the long night of racked, recurrent waking
　　Till the long day,
Fraught with distress brings but the same heartbreaking
　　Front for the fray.

In a far land our Nation's patriots, willing
　　Fought and now lie—
But you—as brave—a harder fate fulfilling,
　　Dare *not* to die!

With the approach of Christmas, we'd relive Dickens' feast and dance given by the employer, old Fezziwig! Old Scrooge was given the power to relive it, too, and now he understood what it meant: Fezziwig had "the power to render us happy or unhappy; to make our service light or burdensome; a pleasure or a toil. Say that this power lies in words and looks; in things so slight and insignificant that it is impossible to add and count 'em up: what then? The happiness he gives is quite as great as if it cost a fortune."

More than once, a passage from Richard Wright's *Black Boy* would tell us things we never knew before about our own country, terrible things. And I remember a poignant letter written by Margaret Fuller about her joy in mother-hood. Mrs. Roosevelt admired that early-nineteenth-century woman, who lived as full an intellectual life as any man in a time that did not encourage such a feat; and when a biography of Fuller was published in 1930, Mrs. Roosevelt contributed an introduction to it.

When Mrs. Roosevelt was asked to read some favorite Frost poems, she concluded with this excerpt from "A Masque of Reason," a poem new to all of us:

Job says there's no such thing as Earth's becoming
An easier place for man to save his soul in.

Except as a hard place to save his soul in
A trial ground where he can try himself
And find out whether he is any good,
It would be meaningless. It might as well
Be Heaven at once and have it over with.

Well!

Just one more favorite, the conclusion to *Wind, Sand and Stars* by Antoine de Saint-Exupéry, a book I believe we all knew and cherished. The author is in a third-class railway carriage sending hundreds of Polish workmen home from France. He sees a peasant child's face and says to himself:

> This is a musician's face. This is the child Mozart. This is a life full of beautiful promise. Little princes in legends are not different from this. Protected, sheltered, cultivated, what could this child become? When my mutation a new rose is born in a garden, all gardeners rejoice. They isolate the rose, tend it, foster it. But there is no gardener for men.

The fire was burning down, but our spirits were challenged beyond a single winter's night.

I WILL NEVER FORGET the first Fourth of July that I heard Mrs. Roosevelt read the Declaration of Independence aloud to us at the poolside after a barbecue at Hyde Park.

When she had reached the end, she continued to read until, like a solemn roll call, she had read the name of each signer.

For the first time, I realized fully the jeopardy in which those men had put their lives and fortunes by committing themselves to the Revolutionary cause.

FAMILY TRADITION also governed the celebration of birthdays. In the Roosevelt tradition, each guest got two candles from the cake. He blew out the first in making a wish for the birthday person, the second in making a wish for himself.

৪৩৪

Eleanor Roosevelt was not fond of having a fuss made over her own birthdays. She was a realist, who believed that "life has got to be lived—that's all there is to it." But she made an exception for her seventieth birthday in October 1954, when the American Association for the United Nations gave a party in her honor. The roster of distinguished guests was evidence of the high esteem in which Mrs. Roosevelt was held by people around the globe. Even Andrei Vishinsky, the famously dour Soviet diplomat with whom Mrs. Roosevelt had clashed over humanitarian issues at the UN in 1946, attended the party.

৪৩৪

MY PARENTS AND I were happy to attend the American Association for the United Nations dinner given on October 11 in honor of Mrs. Roosevelt's seventieth birthday. It was a gala night in the flag-decked grand ballroom of New York's Roosevelt Hotel. A thousand persons had come to applaud Mrs. Roosevelt, who was radiant in a white evening dress, surrounded by her children and friends, associates and acquaintances.

Edward R. Murrow, whose courageous network attack on Senator Joseph P. McCarthy made him more than a distinguished news commentator, was the master of ceremonies. He punctuated a beautifully served and delicious

On the occasion of Eleanor Roosevelt's seventieth birthday: from left to right, Bernard Baruch, William Donner, John Roosevelt, ER, Anna Roosevelt Halsted, James Roosevelt, and Curtis Roosevelt. *(Leo Rosenthal)*

banquet by reading messages from heads of state and world leaders in religion, politics, and the arts.

Henry Morgenthau Jr. said of her: "By her tenderness, her humility, her deep feeling for all humanity, and her zealous faith in the principles of democracy, she has achieved a unique place in history. In the hearts of millions of men and women she has become enshrined as a First Lady—first in the virtues and deeds that are the best expression of womankind."

Harry S Truman wrote: "Mrs. Roosevelt has represented this nation to the world with imagination, grace, charm, good humor and realistic good sense. . . . Mrs. Roosevelt's untiring energy and devotion to the cause of peace and a more enlightened day for mankind have endeared her to us for all time. History will give major recognition to her services."

Tributes from Archibald MacLeish and Helen Keller were also read.

Margaret Truman was present, also Bernard M. Baruch, Senator Herbert H. Lehman, Dean Rusk, Telford Taylor, Dag Hammarskjöld, and Trygve Lie, his predecessor as Secretary-General of the United Nations. More messages followed—from David Ben-Gurion, Pearl S. Buck, and Learned Hand.

The room was darkened to show slides of Mrs. Roosevelt in many lands, at the UN, with children's groups, with workers, with her husband. Each change of subject was received with audible gasps of recognition from the audience. Then, a cartoon drawn especially for the occasion by Herblock was flashed on the screen: A mother aboard a ship approaching our shores points out the Statue of Liberty to her little girl, who replies unhesitatingly, "Of course I know—it's Mrs. Roosevelt." The applause was deafening.

We resumed our dinner and Mr. Murrow read messages from Queen Elizabeth and Prince Philip, from the crowned heads of Sweden, Norway, and Holland; from de Gaulle, and Tito, Nehru, and Churchill. And more messages were read: from Luis Muñoz-Marin, Albert Einstein, Bertrand Russell, Jacques Maritain, and Frank Lloyd Wright.

Clark M. Eichelberger, who, during the dark days of the Battle of Britain, had effectively headed William Allen

White's Committee to Defend America by Aiding the Allies, and was now executive director of the American Association for the United Nations, gave the assembled guests a day-by-day picture of the present work of the guest of honor:

> No one could appreciate Mrs. Roosevelt's unbounded energy until he has been with her through an address to a state board of the AAUN at breakfast, a conference of leaders of the Association in the morning, a luncheon club at noon, a meeting with representatives of many organizations in the afternoon, then a reception, and finally, a huge public meeting at night. And after the night meeting, probably getting ready for an all-night train or plane ride, Mrs. Roosevelt has the same good nature, the same graciousness, as at the first meeting in the morning. She speaks simply. I have never heard her make the same speech on the same subject twice. She has an intuitive quality of adjusting herself to her audience. She can explain the most profound concepts of international relations because she illustrates them with human experiences. She never talks down to an audience; she never talks at it; she talks with it. The audience is part of her, and she is part of it in the great adventure of human experience.

The most dramatic presence at Mrs. Roosevelt's birthday celebration was the unpredictable one of Andrei Vishinsky, permanent delegate for the Soviet Union at the UN. He who had debated her venomously in the General Assembly and who had opposed the Universal Declaration of Human Rights up to the final vote, he who had been so often bested by her serenity or righteous anger, came, smiling and benign, with Madame Vishinsky, proving that not even her deadliest ideological antagonist could resist admiring Mrs. Roosevelt's glowing honesty and total dedication.

At threescore and ten, Mrs. Roosevelt cut her enormous many-tiered birthday cake, and all of us shared it with her. She spoke to the current malaise of our country: "I would like to see us take hold of ourselves, look at ourselves and cease being afraid." More than her achievements, she said, "I treasure the love of my children, the respect of my children, and I would never want my children or my grandchildren to feel that I had failed them." The words were unexpected until they were uttered, but then it was clear that the evening's encomiums were over. Mrs. Roosevelt was in charge. It was getting late and this mother and grandmother had to get home to bed in order to be prepared for the next day's work.

I had spoken to her on the telephone that morning. She had said, "I really don't enjoy this sort of thing, but I suppose it will help the work of the AAUN. At any rate I have put my foot down—there will be no more such celebrations until I'm eighty. *That's* far enough off for me not to have to worry about!"

※

William Turner Levy and Eleanor Roosevelt shared a love of good stories. Many of the stories Mrs. Roosevelt told were about FDR, and about his family and her own. They were both of aristocratic stock, but Franklin was the only child of a doting mother and older father and had had an idyllic childhood, while her childhood had been blighted by an irresponsible though warmhearted father and an unfeeling mother, both of whom died young, leaving her in the care of her strict grandmother Hall.

§◊§

Mrs. Roosevelt's beloved father, Elliott Roosevelt, Theodore Roosevelt's brother, died at the age of thirty-four when his daughter was ten years old. He died in Abingdon, Virginia. No opportunity was made for his daughter to be at the funeral, but for the rest of her life she mourned his loss and venerated his memory.

Her mother had died of diphtheria two years before, and Eleanor was living in the strict and joyless household of her maternal grandmother Hall in New York. To convey the atmosphere of that time, Mrs. Roosevelt once told me, "My great-grandmother, Mrs. Edward H. Ludlow, expected her daughter to visit her every Sunday. One Sunday I went with my Aunt Maude to explain that my grandmother was sick in bed and could not come. My great-grandmother, sitting like a spider at the center of that circle, was furious! She banged her walking stick on the floor, brandished it at us, and told us to tell her daughter she accepted no excuses, none. My grandmother got out of a sickbed and went through the snow to visit her mother. That is the kind of strong-willed head of family, holding the purse strings, that existed in those days. Absolutely heartless and demanding, living by their own rules and expecting everything to be as they willed it."

What a contrast her gentle, sensitive father was. How she looked forward some day to the life together he had pictured for her. "I suppose I have always felt that I missed that period that was promised me as a child."

When she was five, Eleanor went with her father, mother, and little brother to Italy. In the first volume of her autobiography, which she dedicated to the memory of

her father, she recalled a donkey ride she took. She told me
that he read poetry to her, and his love-filled letters were
the joy of her young life. One written at Eastertime in the
last year of his life said, "In a month or six weeks, I will be
back with you and so pleased. I enclose a few white violets,
which you can put in your prayer book at the XXIII Psalm,
and you must know they were Grandmother Roosevelt's
favorite flower." She was his "darling little Nell."

In 1933, Scribner's published *Hunting Big Game in the
Eighties: The Letters of Elliott Roosevelt, Sportsman*, edited by
his daughter, Anna Eleanor Roosevelt. I have a copy presented to me by Mrs. Roosevelt. It was a labor of love and
an attempt to perpetuate his memory. As he writes, he
reveals his sweet and admirable character to the reader.
The tiger he shot was made into a rug to be seen at Val-
Kill Cottage, but there was also the mouse deer he "*could
not* kill" because he observed it "bounding along—stopping for a moment, looking from side to side with such a
funny half innocent, half startled air, then nibbling a
mouthful of grass—suddenly cutting a queer little caper in
apparently excess of joy in living."

Writing about Ceylon, he describes the native hospitals along the road in the upper valley every fourteen
miles, attended by native doctors. He records that no pro-
vision was made, however, for native children. He picked
up three little babies in two days, thrown out on the road
to die. A charitable man at home all his life, he was frus-
trated at not "being able to adopt all the children in Ceylon." He was a father to be proud of.

Mrs. Roosevelt told me that her father was a greater
sportsman than her Uncle Ted. "They would play polo as
though they wanted to kill each other!" A sudden thought

struck her. "You do know, of course, that he was Franklin's godfather."

Mrs. Roosevelt was unable to dissemble. "It is a terrible thing to say," she confided to me in one of our late-night talks, "but I hated my mother. She was disappointed in my looks and said so. She was not satisfied by anything that I did. She would speak harshly to me—and in front of the servants and visitors, too—often calling me 'Granny' derisively. I remember once in regard to my eating sugar, so much was made of it—she had a way of going on forever. And, of course, although she had reason, she made clear her coldness toward my beloved father."

In the so-called cross room, a room that joined areas upstairs in Val-Kill Cottage, was a several-feet-high photographic portrait of her mother. Mrs. Roosevelt never harbored animosities. Guests were occasionally surprised to see crystal or linen with her mother-in-law's initials, SDR.

One night late in summer on the way up to bed, she stopped, standing in front of an old hunting print in a frame that represented an English country fence, and mused, "I don't think people change. . . . We must learn to accept them as they are." I was struck by the intense thoughtfulness of her expression.

Remembering her brother Hall's death, she spoke of his terrible labored breathing in the hours before the end. As in her father's case, alcohol was a strongly contributing factor. She shook her head, but brightened suddenly and added, "His generosity and brilliance! You would have liked him, Bill. You'd have had much in common."

The last time Mrs. Roosevelt was well enough to have me for dinner, the evening ended with our speaking of her father. She took me into her bedroom to show me her father's copy of the New Testament. She removed it from the bedside table. We sat down on the bed and she pointed out passages that he had marked. Then she showed me a lock of her hair he had kept in it. The volume was falling apart and she wanted my advice on how to best preserve it. Should she have it rebound? Could I recommend a reliable place? I told her that to some extent rebinding inevitably destroys the authentic feel, the "personality" of the book. I didn't think the result would please her because it would be too altered. Then I reminded her that I had her child-hood copy of the New Testament in French and had pre-served it by having it enclosed in linen boards that fitted snugly into a matching slipcase box. She remembered it at once. Yes, that would keep it intact and protect it at the same time. That's what we would do. She asked me to take charge of it.

Mrs. Roosevelt told me that when the news of her father's death reached New York, she was not told at once, but knew something dreadful had happened. There was whispering in corners.

"He had died in the house of his mistress. The family was flabbergasted, but there was overt relief, too! He was judged damned. They got the funeral over with as quickly as possible. That woman had informed the family and they arranged to have him taken to an undertaker and she was never a part of what followed. But *she* had been taking care of him when they would have no part of him! I was treated like the daughter of a wicked, ruined man. But you're a clergyman. What do *you* say? Can he be forgiven by God?"

Reassurance was simple. I said to her, "Can he be for-given by God? I couldn't keep him out of heaven for that, and God must be much more generous than I, or none of us stand a chance of getting there." She smiled. At the last service we attended together we sang, and I could hear in her voice:

> Blest Saviour, then in love,
> Fear and distrust remove,
> O bear me safe above,
> A ransomed soul.
> Amen.

ON ANOTHER OCCASION, I was able to tell Mrs. Roosevelt a remarkable story about her uncle, Theodore Roosevelt, that she had not known and that greatly interested her. I heard the story from Dr. Charles Mendelsohn, a history teacher at Townsend Harris Preparatory School in New York, where I was a student.

Dr. Mendelsohn was standing in the crowd outside the Republican convention hall in Philadelphia, having attended the day's proceedings, just after Theodore Roosevelt had been nominated the vice presidential candidate. "I was next to his carriage, not six feet from Mr. Roosevelt," he said in his understated way, "and the tears were pouring down Roosevelt's cheeks. Never had I seen a man so broken, for, as you must realize, to become vice president of the United States then was absolute death: His party had shelved him!" Of course, it was only a matter of months until fate decided otherwise with the assassination of President McKinley.

໌

If it was her public activism on behalf of others that drew acclaim, it was her private life that Eleanor Roosevelt cherished above all. In the midst of all the tributes at her seventieth birthday party, she declared that above all her achievements, she

Mrs. R loved her children and grandchildren and never wanted them to feel she had failed them: at Val-Kill Pond with Tamas, Sally, Fala, and Nina. *(Cowles Magazines, Inc.)*

prized "the love of my children, the respect of my children"; she would never want her children or grandchildren to feel that she had failed them. Until the end of her life, she was a loving and engaged parent, and—in the face of the marital and other vicissitudes of her children—a remarkably nonjudgmental one. William Turner Levy was struck by her devotion to the memory of her third baby, who had died at seven months, and by the way she handled her argumentative, if affectionate, adult sons.

❧

Although it was a chilly weekend, Mrs. Roosevelt and I swam several lengths of the pool in the temporary sun before lunch or dinner on three occasions. Mrs. Roosevelt would poise herself on the end of the diving board, extend her arms, fingertips touching, close her eyes—and plunge. "I was mortally afraid of water," she told me one late afternoon as we walked back to the house after a swim. "Uncle Ted just pushed me in, sink or swim, and I was terrified as a little girl. I used to pray for rainy days when I stayed in his home at Oyster Bay. Then, instead of tramping off across the dunes and into the water, Uncle Ted would take us up to his gun room in the tower and read aloud from the Norse sagas and the *Chanson de Roland*."

"But," I said to Mrs. Roosevelt, "you not only swim now, you even *dive*!"

"I felt I had to learn to swim when my children were growing up because I had to be with them at the water, and I might have to rescue them, so I took lessons at the Y and learned. I was scared to death of the water, but there are certain things you must force yourself to do. I'm still scared of the water, but I cannot give in to an absolutely irrational fear."

ON MORE THAN ONE occasion when Mrs. Roosevelt was being interviewed and reference was made to her five children, I heard her sober correction: "You are mistaken. I have had six children. Our third child, baby Franklin, died of a weakened heart brought on by influenza shortly before reaching the age of eight months."

The reporters saw no story here—they filed it, if at all, as a statistic. But Mrs. Roosevelt was a mother. She once took me to see his tiny gravestone in the churchyard next to Saint James's in Hyde Park.

"He was a big, beautiful boy," was all she could say.

SEVERAL TIMES over the years a heated discussion after dinner at Hyde Park led to a violent argument, usually involving two or more of the Roosevelt sons. They were very fond of each other, and all four always greeted each other with a hug and kiss. I told Mrs. Roosevelt how wonderful I found that freedom in expressing their love for each other. She agreed, "They became used to that as boys because Franklin always hugged and kissed them, so they're not in the least self-conscious."

Nevertheless, they did have volatile tempers upon occasion, but what struck me was their mother's reaction. She would do one of two things to isolate herself from the conflict: take out a deck of cards and begin playing solitaire (I suspect the deck was never otherwise used), or pick up a newspaper, open it fully, and disappear behind it (once I was vastly amused to notice that it was upside down!).

Chapter 9

Discovering Mrs. Roosevelt

*W*ILLIAM TURNER LEVY *discovered that Eleanor Roosevelt was a person who made a deep impression on almost everyone she met, not simply because of who she was but because of what she was. And although human beings often reveal different facets of themselves to different people, the impression she made on people was remarkably consistent. In the ten years of their friendship, William Turner Levy learned much about Mrs. Roosevelt from the stories her friends told. Some of them were amusing, but most were tributes to the profound humanity of this remarkable woman.*

Stories that Mrs. Roosevelt told about herself deepened William Turner Levy's understanding of her qualities of mind and heart. She was never pretentious. She had that most desirable of traits, and one not always found in the prominent: the ability to laugh at herself. She did not hesitate to relate anecdotes about pecadillos in her past. Other stories enhanced William Turner Levy's awareness of her intense compassion for others.

☙❧

HAVING JUST RETURNED to the United States via Europe, Mrs. Roosevelt wrote to say, "Those postcards were the loveliest things I have ever seen and I was delighted to get them and your nice letter in Paris." Mrs. Roosevelt, obviously, had been nostalgically touched by the collection of New England scenes. "I am so glad your holiday has, as usual, been so perfect in Vermont," she continued, "and I am particularly happy you saw (or were going to see) Dorothy Canfield Fisher."

Mrs. Roosevelt had a warm admiration for the Vermont novelist, a deeply rooted old-fashioned American who gave generously of her time, abilities, and money to help a wide range of young people, from English wartime refugees to students in American Negro colleges. Dorothy Canfield Fisher had told my parents and me during this recent visit: "The image I have when I think of Mrs. Roosevelt comes out of my childhood recollections of artists' representations of the Good Fairy. I see a dusty, cobwebbed room. Scorpions, scaly snakes, and menacing bats inhabit its dark corners. Mrs. Roosevelt, the spirit of goodness, enters. She walks right through the filth of accumulated prejudices and absurdities—and all is illuminated with light and all the horrid creatures can be heard scurrying away. She passes on, leaving a clean place to dwell in, the ends of her long skirt having flicked away the last particle of foulness. Everything evil shrivels up in her presence!"

MRS. ROOSEVELT WAS the subject of one of innumerable conversations between Lorena Hickok and myself. I cannot recall how we once got on the subject of guns.

Miss Hickok told me, "The Secret Service insisted that Mrs. Roosevelt carry a gun during the White House years, so she carried it, but empty of ammunition and locked in the glove compartment of the car when we traveled—lest the children get at it. Later, in New York, she had no pistol at all. For one thing, in New York, you had to be fingerprinted annually for the permit—and Mrs. Roosevelt shrugged that off with, 'It would get my hands dirty!' Can't you just hear her? Any excuse would do!"

Miss Hickok—"Hick" to all of us whom she liked—suddenly remembered something: "Mrs. Roosevelt used to carry a teargas pen in her pocketbook when she was with FDR. 'I could stand with my back to him and fire it,' she announced with determination. I didn't have the heart to tell her that she could never have got at it in time in that crowded pocketbook of hers!"

My warm and dramatic friend, the novelist Fannie Hurst, shared another illuminating story about Mrs. Roosevelt. They were both scheduled to appear on the dais at a charity function in New York. Miss Hurst, seeing an opportunity to spend a little more time with Mrs. Roosevelt, suggested that they might share a taxi. Mrs. Roosevelt agreed and Miss Hurst picked her up at the appointed time.

When they had gone only a few blocks, Mrs. Roosevelt exclaimed, "Oh, I'm *so* sorry, Miss Hurst, but we shall have to go back. I forgot something."

Miss Hurst was secretly pleased that they would be spending even more time together. After returning to the taxi, Mrs. Roosevelt apologized again, produced an engraved card from her evening purse and said, "You see, we had to go back—because I forgot my invitation."

Fannie enjoyed my appreciation of the story, smiled wryly, and said, "I must confess that if I had forgotten my invitation, I'd not have gone back for it!"

In a similar vein, Mrs. Roosevelt's dear friend and personal physician, Dr. David Gurewitsch, told me that when their plane was positioning itself to land at Karachi in 1952, Mrs. Roosevelt looked out the window at a crowd in the millions and said to him, "Look, David, someone *very* important must be arriving today!" Dr. Gurewitsch added that he would only tell this to me because I would recognize its ingenuousness: "I wouldn't care to tell it to a doubter."

T. S. Eliot said, "Humility is endless."

YET ANOTHER STORY conveys vividly just how Mrs. Roosevelt impressed people. One evening she and I emerged from a Broadway theater and went directly to my car in the parking lot next door.

I saw at once that the entrance was being blocked by four drunks, two men and two women, who were shouting obscenities and standing in the way of cars. The lot attendants were unable to cope with them. One of the women brandished a half-empty bottle and let out a roar of drunken laughter.

I wondered if we should retreat, and feared that they would recognize Mrs. Roosevelt, but she walked right through the confusion.

One of the women recognized her, became cold sober, began to shake the others by their arms, and kept trying to enunciate, "It's Mss. Rooooosevelt, it's Mss. Rooooosevelt!"

By the time we got in the car and up to the entrance, the four of them were standing in line and swaying in our direction. One of the men doffed his cap and all four muttered, "God blesh you, Mss. Rooooosevelt. God blesh you!"

I GREW ACCUSTOMED to seeing strangers greet Mrs. Roosevelt, smile, say a word, shake a hand. The depth of feeling in their eyes conveyed years of gratitude. Those in wheelchairs or otherwise seeming in need of a little extra pat on the shoulder received it along with an encouraging word and understanding look.

No letter went unanswered. An acquaintance or colleague, in most cases decades after receiving it, would tell me exactly what it said or bring it in to show me, a family treasure. "I was only twelve years old when I wrote to her about my troubles with my schoolwork." "It was after my dog had died."

It was a two-way street. Mrs. Roosevelt told me that during a New York blizzard she couldn't find a taxi, so, not to be late for her appointment, she ducked down into the subway. It was jammed. Several gentlemen at once offered their seats. She busied herself with her newspaper. Two station stops later, a young Black woman heading for the door paused, selected a flower from a bouquet in her hand, and presented it to Mrs. Roosevelt.

"Wasn't that the sweetest thing imaginable?" she asked me, clearly equating it with her honorary degree from Oxford.

And she was right. Once at Hyde Park, I saw for the first time in the cross room upstairs, a framed reproduction of Holbein's portrait of Erasmus. It prompted me to tell Mrs. Roosevelt the story that once, when the great man was entering a cathedral, a woman approached him and told him how blessed he was, having translated the New Testament into Latin. "What a service to our Lord," she exclaimed. Erasmus thanked her, turned, and pointed to a peasant woman in the act of lighting a candle. "No more a service than that woman's. I did what I was able, and so does she."

Mrs. Roosevelt spent herself to enhance the lives of others. After her death, my friend Reinhold Niebuhr, one of the great theologians of this age, wrote to me: "She was a saint in both the classic and the modern sense."

AT DINNER ONE EVENING at Mrs. Roosevelt's home in New York, the subject of costumes came up. Most of us had funny or embarrassing memories. When we had exhausted our store, I somewhat boldly asked our hostess if she had a story for us.

"As a matter of fact, I was thinking, as you were talking, about a rather elaborate costume party in the White House. I can't for the life of me remember what the occasion was, but the theme must have been the Gilbert and Sullivan operas since Franklin was dressed as the Pirate King in "The Pirates of Penzance"—he just loved it!—and I remember that Admiral Byrd was, appropriately enough, the Admiral in "H.M.S. Pinafore."

"And what part did you assume?" I asked.

"I don't remember—I was busy dressing the others!"

"THIS WILL AMUSE YOU, William." I could see it had already amused Mrs. Roosevelt. "In New York the other day, two police department detectives arrived just as I was preparing to leave the house. They asked to come in and, as I was putting on my hat and gathering my papers and things, at my request they sat . . . on those little red chairs by my couch-bed in the dressing room—burly men full of 'Yes, ma'am's. It was an incongruous sight—those *big* men on those *little* chairs. One of them was holding a postcard between his thumb and index finger, as if it were about to explode. 'Ma'am, it says 'Eleanor Roosevelt will die on Saturday!' 'Oh,' said I, 'so that's why you're here. But I don't need any protection. Today's Monday!'

"Once on the street, we discovered that their police car had delayed a garbage truck waiting to make its pickup. I apologized to the two garbagemen, who joined in saying with happy smiles, 'Anytime! For Mrs. Roosevelt—anytime!' Isn't that delicious?"

I LOVED MRS. ROOSEVELT'S unwillingness to end a day, to prolong it by a late-night glass of milk or piece of fruit while sharing thoughts; it reaffirmed her sense of the value of time.

On one such occasion she told me about a visit she had made as a child to her nearby Aunt Laura, who was an Astor. "Not unusually for me at that age, I must have been caught up in the book I was reading before lunch and did not hear the gong which, on the Astor estate, always announced lunch a half hour in advance. That gave the family and any guests time to end a stroll on the grounds overlooking the Hudson, or end a game, enter the house, and wash their hands. Suddenly, I became aware that it had grown quiet and that it must indeed be lunchtime. I returned to my room and made myself presentable, only to find upon entering the dining room that grace had been said and soup started. Chagrined, I approached my aunt, who was seated at the head of the table, curtseyed, and said sheepishly, 'I'm sorry. I didn't have enough time.' Stern Aunt Laura replied with a memorable dictum: "You had all the time there was!"

Mrs. Roosevelt agreed that that was an irreducible truth.

Mrs. Roosevelt told me, with a disarming laugh at herself, of a visit to Buckingham Palace during World War II.

An equerry had escorted her to the king's office for her audience. "It is an immense palace with seemingly endless corridors," she said. "Well, when I had completed reporting to the king on certain matters, and answering his questions, I excused myself so that no act of courtesy on his part might keep him from his many wartime duties. Once out in the corridor, I realized that I hadn't the slightest idea how to get to the main gate! I pursued what *seemed* a reasonable direction, but apparently made all the wrong turns. I was lost. An equerry rushed up to me and asked what I was doing! 'I'm trying to find my way out,' said I, 'for I've completed my business with the king.' 'But, Madame,' he stammered, incredulous, 'no one ever leaves the king. The king leaves them.' For a moment I was transported back across the years . . . and, under the sting of the reprimand, I felt like a very naughty child."

Mrs. Roosevelt's right leg was bandaged!

"What happened to you?" I blurted out.

"Oh, I was hit by a taxicab. It's nothing serious, mostly a sprained ankle, but it hurts like blazes! The driver got out of the taxi and, recognizing me, was distraught—though I doubt that's the word he would have used. What a predicament he was in! I told him I was unhurt, but he hovered sympathetically, so I raised my voice and said,

After Mrs. R's altercation with the taxicab, when she told the driver to drive away before anyone saw him— so he wouldn't lose his job. At Hyde Park with Averell Harriman (left) and myself. *(Courtesy of William Turner Levy)*

'Go, go, drive away quickly before someone sees you!' I think I may have frightened him! But you realize, he could have lost his job!"

ONE EVENING AFTER DINNER in our Riverdale apartment, the reminiscences of my parents brought to mind two poignant memories of Mrs. Roosevelt's which she shared with us.

Time had not erased her sense of sadness at having once seen, in a factory where artificial flowers were made for ladies' hats, little girls with little hands who had worked for so many hours, they fell off their benches from exhaustion. The need for child labor laws had, in 1915, inspired Sarah Cleghorn's quatrain:

> The golf links lie so near the mill
>   That almost every day
> The laboring children can look out
>   And watch the men at play.

The constitutional amendment regarding minimum work age passed by the Congress in 1924 was not approved by enough states to become the law of the land; not until 1938 was a sixteen-year-old minimum age set for children, and then, being a federal act, it only applied to work produced for interstate or foreign commerce.

Nor could Mrs. Roosevelt forget, working for the Red Cross in Washington during World War I, the visits she made to wards in military hospitals, and the funerals she was detailed to attend in Arlington Cemetery, bringing flowers, when only a few or no family members could be present. "To attend the burial service of a stranger is to be joined to another in an undeniably significant fashion."

Men alive today, who in World War II were burnt into facelessness by explosives, recall Mrs. Roosevelt, brushing hospital advice aside and striding through the doors and into the stench and horror of the burn ward to personally pin on each man's hospital jacket, on behalf of the President of the United States, the Order of the Purple Heart.

❦

Mrs. R couldn't wait to try on the gorgeous red academic gown that came along with her honorary degree from Oxford and insisted that I capture the event on film. *(Courtesy of William Turner Levy)*

Always, Eleanor Roosevelt wore her fame lightly, and yet she could take honest pride in public recognition of her accomplishments. One memorable day she modeled for William Turner Levy the newly arrived Oxford academic gown symbolizing her honorary Doctor of Civil Law degree from that distinguished university.

৪৩৪

In brilliant sunlight and proud as a peacock, Mrs. Roosevelt in her gorgeous red Oxford academic gown swept up to the table I was using as a desk in the garden at Val-Kill Cottage.

"Isn't it glorious?" she cooed.

"Smashing," I replied, joining her mood.

"It has just arrived," she told me. "They didn't have one when I was awarded the degree during the war, all looms were making uniforms! Now, it's a wonderful surprise."

"Let me get my camera," I said. "We must record this historic moment!"

When I returned, she had placed the accompanying black velvet beret on her head to complete the effect.

"Just think, William, I have a Doctor of Civil Laws degree—although I never went to college!"

"That's right," I said, focusing the camera, "you got it the hard way."

Chapter 10

Discovering FDR

PERHAPS IT WAS her early experience of sorrow that gave Mrs. Roosevelt her forbearance and compassion. She did not hesitate to condemn acts of injustice and unkindness, but she rarely complained when these were directed against her. Her own husband had been the source of enormous hurt in their marriage, but her reminiscences of FDR and their life together were consistently admiring and affectionate. She clearly agreed with Churchill's perspective of FDR's role in world history.

As she had remained loyal to him in life, so Eleanor Roosevelt remained loyal to her husband in death. On his birthday, as William Turner Levy discovered, it was her practice to take flowers to his grave in the Rose Garden and weave them, after a prayer, into an elaborate floral design.

⊗

MRS. ROOSEVELT INVITED Sir Campbell Stuart for dinner at Val-Kill Cottage and invited me for the weekend because she felt that it would be an opportunity I would value. As treasurer of the committee to create a memorial to FDR in England, Sir Campbell Stuart was responsible for the brunt of the work.

A year before, Mrs. Roosevelt had given me a copy of the beautifully produced forty-five-page "Order of Ceremony at the Unveiling of the Memorial to President Roosevelt by Mrs. Roosevelt in Grosvenor Square, London, Monday, April 12th, 1948." It was the sort of brilliant national occasion of celebration at which the English excel: the participation of their majesties King George VI and Queen Elizabeth and of Queen Mary, the Queen Mother; the benediction from the Most Reverend the Lord Archbishop of Canterbury, the presence of President Truman's personal representative, Ambassador Henry S. Hooker, a lifetime friend of President Roosevelt; the Band and Buglers of the Royal Marines; the contingent of the United States Marine Corps, sent over by President Truman; the glorious music of the national anthems, Sousa's march "The Stars and Stripes Forever," Sir William Walton's march "Crown Imperial," and all present singing "The Battle Hymn of the Republic."

The Duke of Westminster had surrendered all rights to Grosvenor Square, and the funds to create a garden and raise the statue were collected by an appeal to the hearts of the people of Britain.

Sir Campbell Stuart told me that the prime minister, Clement Attlee, and Winston Churchill had launched the campaign on radio. The contributions rolled in, in shillings, with a maximum of five shillings from any individual. The appeal was quickly closed, having been so magnificently supported.

The unveiling ceremony took place at eleven in the morning. That evening, the date was April 12, a dinner

A

Merry
Christmas
and a
Happy
New Year
from
william
Turner
Levy

19   58

For my 1958 Christmas card, when I asked Mrs. R if I could use some of the words she spoke in London on the occasion of the unveiling of her husband's statue in Grosvenor Square, she immediately agreed and added her signature. The card's interior is shown on following pages. *(Courtesy of William Turner Levy)*

was given in honor of Mrs. Roosevelt at the Savoy Hotel. The guest list of about one thousand included the most distinguished members of English society, civilian and military, headed by members of the royal family.

I thank Mrs Franklin D. Roosevelt
for permission to send you these
words she spoke in London in 1948
upon the occasion of the unveiling
of her husband's statue in
Grosvenor Square.

I asked Sir Campbell Stuart for his most indelible memory of the day. "The words spoken by His Majesty just before he invited Mrs. Roosevelt to unveil the monument by pulling a cord which released the Union Jack," he replied. "I was struck by their simplicity. It was perfectly clear he had written the brief address himself. It was a tribute from his heart. He spoke of the hospitality he and the queen received in the United States and how they had looked forward to a visit the Roosevelts had planned to

The pure in heart
  are free from suspicion.
The great and humble
  cannot be humiliated.
Pray God we join together
and invite all others to join us
in creating a world
where justice, truth
  and good faith rule.

Eleanor Roosevelt

meet the British people. The king deeply regretted that opportunity for the President to experience in person the love the English people had for him was denied by his untimely death. The king spoke from a sense of personal loss, and it made his simple words terribly moving. Then, as soon as the monument was revealed, the Royal Marines played the 'Star-Spangled Banner.' I do not think there was a dry eye in Grosvenor Square. The king's shadow fell upon the shaft as he placed his wreath on the monument."

Time was erased as Sir Campbell Stuart spoke and there were again tears in his eyes.

When I asked Mrs. Roosevelt later that evening about her primary memory of the day, she answered, without hesitation, "What Mr. Churchill said about the President at the dinner. I don't trust my memory, and his language was so eloquent. Let me read it to you. It will take just a moment to get the program; it's on my desk."

I knew she didn't like being waited on, so I made no offer to get it for her. She returned with it open to the page. She had her glasses on and she began reading. "In Roosevelt's life and by his action he changed, he altered decisively and permanently, the social axis, the moral axis, of mankind by involving the New World inexorably and irrevocably in the fortunes of the Old. His life must, therefore, be regarded as one of the commanding events in human destiny."

Mrs. Roosevelt looked up, removed her glasses, and said, "I found that important because Mr. Churchill was speaking as an historian and placing Franklin in the perspective of history."

Later, when I retired, I took the program up to my room to read Churchill's entire speech, including the part that Mrs. Roosevelt did not read: "We must ascribe to Mrs. Roosevelt the marvellous fact that a crippled man, the victim of a cruel affliction, was able for more than ten years to ride the storms of peace and war at the summit of the United States. The debt that we owe to President Roosevelt is also owed to her. I am sure that she feels around her to-night, in this old parent land and in this great company, the esteem and the affection of the whole British people."

MRS. ROOSEVELT FONDLY RECALLED the quickness of her husband's mind. The Roosevelts made a practice of attending the theater regularly in Washington when the New York productions took to the road and appeared at the National Theatre. They also frequently invited the casts to the White House for supper afterward.

The night they saw the Lindsay and Crouse play *Life with Father*, based on the Clarence Day novel, their guests naturally included the youngsters in the cast. FDR was entertaining the youngest boy by pointing out the George Washington portrait that had been rescued by Dolley Madison when the British had set the White House on fire during the War of 1812.

Mrs. Roosevelt told me, "Franklin played up the drama of the story—as he could do *so* well—and we were all ears. He said, 'Dolley Madison cut it out of the frame, rolled it up, and fled—just as the British soldiers appeared!' In the pause that followed, the boyish voice piped up, 'How did she cut it out, Mr. President?'

"I was always astounded that Franklin knew so much about historical things. Now, I was certain, he was stumped at last—but not a bit of it! He replied with absolute aplomb. 'Why, with a knife from the kitchen, of course!' I was momentarily taken aback, but immediately joined the laughter."

ANOTHER FAVORITE MEMORY was of the British royal visit in 1939. The American people were electrified by the first visit to American shores of a British king. Their Majesties King George VI and Queen Elizabeth were the nation's guests at the invitation of President and Mrs. Roosevelt. Without question, the best-remembered event, as far as the public was concerned, was the hot dog picnic at Hyde Park, the twelve-hundred-acre estate of the Roosevelts.

During the planning stages, the President was asked if he thought the collection of naval prints in the entrance hall of the Hyde Park home, many from the time of the American Revolution and filled with anti-British caricatures, should be removed in deference to the king. Mrs. Roosevelt told me, "My husband's reply was, 'I think he'll enjoy them!' And he did!"

There's an irreverent footnote to the visit that I learned, not from Mrs. Roosevelt but from a faithful and trustworthy member of the domestic staff at Hyde Park. It concerned a toilet seat.

Although frugal, the President's mother, Sara Delano Roosevelt, decided that a new toilet seat would look better in the queen's bathroom, so she ordered one from the proprietor of a local hardware store.

After the departure of the royal guests, she decided that the old seat still had some years of wear in it, so she returned the hardly used new seat for a credit to her account. Now, the proprietor was a frugal Yankee too and refused to accept the arrangement, but Sara Delano Roosevelt was adamant. He felt it useless to argue with her, so he deferred to his longtime customer—but he was not going to be out-of-pocket! He displayed the contested seat in his window. The "For Sale" sign included the information that it was a rarity since it had been used by Her Britannic Majesty Queen Elizabeth!

Word quickly reached his valued customer, who had a sudden change of mind. She could indeed, she told him, use the toilet seat and would accept the original billing.

Royal visits were not unusual occurrences at Val-Kill. In addition to the British monarchs and Queen Wilhelmina of the Netherlands, H.R.H. Princess Julianna of the Netherlands paid a visit for a picnic lunch with Mrs. R and President Roosevelt in 1943. *(Courtesy of the Franklin D. Roosevelt Library)*

ANOTHER ROYAL VISIT also provided one of Mrs. Roosevelt's favorite funny stories—about Hyde Park mosquitoes and a queen! "My husband could sometimes be very exasperating. For example, he stoutly maintained that, 'One of the advantages of this area is that you don't need screens. Mosquitoes don't exist on the Hudson!' So he didn't screen the porch at Top Cottage, the retreat he built high up on the property as a place where he could get away from the big house if he wanted to. I remember one hot evening in the summer when we were sitting on his porch with Queen Wilhelmina. Well, I could see that her ankles were being cruelly bitten by mosquitoes. When she mentioned the word 'mosquito,' Franklin brushed it aside, smiled with irritating insouciance, and maintained that 'We don't have mosquitoes here—they just don't exist!' The portly queen tried in vain to pull her skirts down lower over her large legs, which had become a prime target area, and chose every moment when Franklin looked away to shoo off the bloodthirsty insects. I don't know whether Franklin was immune to the bites or the polio had somehow left him unable to feel them. I knew I couldn't move him indoors, but I marched into the house and brought out a heavy woolen blanket—all I could find—and the queen gratefully covered her legs. Franklin took no apparent notice."

ON ONE OCCASION, I had written Mrs. Roosevelt to say that I didn't think I remembered the exact words of an anecdote she had told me. Had I gotten it right? Would she repeat it? She responded promptly: "It is true that I did go up to Franklin's room and say, 'Sometimes I wonder whether people are worth saving,' but his answer was not, 'Sleep on that, Eleanor,' but, 'Give people time, my dear. It takes time to understand things. You are much too impatient and would never make a good politician.' I don't think I have used this story and you are quite welcome to use it."

In a later letter from Mrs. Roosevelt, she expressed pleasure in my finding a large color print of the President's portrait by Frank O. Salisbury, identical to the one she had in her bedroom at Hyde Park. She was also pleased that I had been able to purchase a set of four leatherbound books from FDR's collection of miniatures that were inscribed by the President, "The Chancellor's Copy." (FDR collected stamps and naval prints as well as miniature books.) Mrs. Roosevelt explained that "the Chancellor" was Robert R. Livingston, her ancestor, who administered the oath of office to George Washington.

Upon further research, I discovered that Mrs. Roosevelt was descended from an illustrious family of statesmen, diplomats, and jurists. As the first chancellor of the State of New York, Livingston (1746–1813) had indeed administered the presidential oath to Washington. He had also been a member of both the Continental Congress and the committee to draft the Declaration of Independence, but had not signed it because the New York provincial congress had not authorized him to do so. He was the first secretary of the new nation's Department of Foreign Affairs and, as such, issued the orders for the commissioners to negotiate the peace treaty at the end of the Revolution. Later, Jefferson had named him minister to France, and he conducted the negotiations that led to the Louisiana Purchase. He also financed the experiments of Robert Fulton, who named the first commercially successful steamboat after Livingston's home on the Hudson, the *Clermont*.

The four volumes are works in French by de Florian: each volume has a bookplate elaborately engraved with the words "Robt. R. Livingston, Esqr. of Clermont" and the motto *Spero meliora* ("Hope for better things"). One volume had, as a bookmark, a copy of the chancellor's Revolutionary calling card engraved with his name, a rifle, and the words *Ei utilis qui uti scit* ("Useful to him who knows how to use it"). These had been passed down in Mrs.

Roosevelt's family, and she had given them to her husband for his collection.

Exchanging letters had by now become a habit; in addition, I sent Mrs. Roosevelt, as a Christmas card, T. S. Eliot's new and separately printed poem, "The Cultivation of Christmas Trees."

I was deeply touched when she telephoned me on New Year's Eve: "It is so nice to be thinking of special people tonight!" she said. "And I have read and reread Mr. Eliot's charming Christmas poem. Thank you so much for your many kindnesses to me this year."

As Mrs. Roosevelt was speaking, my eyes rested upon a brilliant poinsettia plant that she had sent, timed to arrive on Christmas Eve.

ONE WEEKEND, Mrs. Roosevelt drove me to the Vanderbilt estate grounds. She parked the car on a bluff overlooking the river and showed me FDR's favorite view of the Hudson. It was north of the mansion and a tiny, wooded island offshore added to the serenity of the scene.

I noticed once again the loving inflection in her voice when she said her husband's first name; as she spoke it, there seemed to be more than the two syllables.

"He loved the slow-moving water," his widow told me. "It had, I think, back in his boyhood, entered his bloodstream, always a comforting and reassuring presence. Absorbing the atmosphere of a tranquil place, retelling a story out of his quieter past or that of his parents, reading a detective story, working on his stamp collection, writing his name in his books—he particularly sought these activities when he was perplexed or weary, and I never saw them fail to restore his vitality and spirits. Another sure cure for overwork was for us to go off for a picnic lunch on the spur of the moment!"

She paused, reflectively. "It was especially difficult for a wartime president to escape the confines of the White House. I remember one afternoon during the war Franklin begged the Secret Service to let him drive a short way out of Washington to a restaurant called Normandy Farms. 'Nobody will expect us,' he said, 'and furthermore it's a quiet, rainy Saturday afternoon between lunch and dinner. They'll light a fire for us and we can have tea.' The Secret Service relented, following him with only one car of agents. They peeked into the restaurant, found it empty except for a few waitresses setting tables, and so we entered. The waitress nearest the door looked wide-eyed at Franklin and, without saying a word, promptly dropped her tray of dishes! Franklin was *so* amused! I remember that Hick was with us. We had a quiet hour by the fire, chatting and having tea and cinammon toast. It did Franklin the world of good. At times, he said, he really felt like a prisoner."

The next day, before I left for New York, Mrs. Roosevelt knocked at my open door while I was packing. In her hand was a large sheet of heavy paper, light tan in color, bearing the seal of New York at the top and a text in the facsimile handwriting of Franklin Delano Roosevelt.

"I found this most fortuitously, and thought that you would like to have it. It's a copy of Franklin's Thanksgiving Day proclamation in 1930. He had some printed to use as Christmas gifts that year. It must be quite rare because as paper, it's fragile, and as pre-Presidential, it was probably not greatly valued." I read it then and there and told her I would frame it for my room.

She complied with my request for an inscription, writing: "Given to William Turner Levy by Eleanor Roosevelt, June 25, 1955." The proclamation reads:

State of New York
Executive Chamber

For generations past it has been the custom in families, in communities and in churches, in the autumn of the year to give thanks to the Supreme Creator for the blessings bestowed by Him upon mankind. At this time also we offer prayers for a continuation of His Divine Favor.

Now, therefore, I, Franklin D. Roosevelt, Governor of the State of New York, do proclaim Thursday, the twenty-seventh day of November in this year of our Lord One Thousand nine hundred and thirty as

Thanksgiving Day.

Let the people of our State on that day give thanks and pray to Almighty God who has given us this good land for our heritage, that we may prove ourselves a people mindful of His favor and glad to do His will; that He may bless our land with honorable industry, sound learning, and pure manners; that He may save us from violence, discord and confusion; from pride and arrogancy, and from every evil way; that He may defend our liberties, and fashion into one united people the multitudes brought hither out of many kindreds and tongues; that He may endue with the spirit of wisdom those to whom we entrust the authority of government, that there be justice and peace at home; that in the time of prosperity, He may fill our hearts with thankfulness, and in the day of trouble, suffer not our trust in Him to fail.

Franklin D. Roosevelt

LATER, AT HOME, reflecting upon Mrs. Roosevelt's photograph, I recalled discussing with her, when I first asked for it, the problem of obtaining a good likeness by the camera lens, which captures only a fleeting second of one's changing countenance. But we agreed that the advantage of an artist's portrait, which ideally captures one's essence rather than the look of a moment, is nullified if the artist is less than a master.

"Finally," she had said, "I suppose all that matters is that someone who cares for you is satisfied that the resemblance evokes a quality he or she admires in you." She told me that few things in her travels had moved her more than constantly finding her husband's picture posted or pinned up in the homes—sometimes mere huts, almost hovels—of simple people in many parts of the world. "They felt close to Franklin, and recognized in him their champion," she concluded, gravely but proudly.

In the course of my research, I discovered among the President's books at Hyde Park several volumes endearingly inscribed to his longtime personal secretary Marguerite Le Hand, known to the Roosevelt family as "Missy." I asked Mrs. Roosevelt about them. I told her that they were the only books I had ever seen inscribed in such a manner except those signed to herself.

Mrs. Roosevelt told me, "When Missy died, she left all her books and papers to the library, and we are fortunate to have them, as you know. Your surmise is right. Franklin loved Missy. He couldn't have lived without me, but neither could he have lived without Missy. She became fine and he was fine, so it was all right. If he had met her earlier, it would have been different. . . ."

FDR was a man of many facets and he required many around him to respond to what he found unique in each. No single individual could be all-in-all to him. He might shape policy with the help of one and merely play poker with another. Their loyalty sustained him. During the last presidential campaign he got soaked riding in an open car during a downpour in a political parade in New York. When he arrived at his wife's house in Greenwich Village, she drew a hot tub for him, saying, "You must be frozen," for it was winter. "Not at all," he answered. "Their love kept me warm." He had continued the ride through the crowded streets because the American people were waiting to see their President—and because his political opponents were questioning his physical stamina.

On this occasion, Mrs. Roosevelt also talked about his attractiveness to women. "He was particularly attracted to women and they often misunderstood his appreciation of their company. A crown princess or a charming British lady might end up at his feet during cocktails, popping an occasional hors d'oeuvre in his mouth. A few days later I'd get a telephone call. 'Babs, you must come right back and get rid of her—this is getting out of hand!' He could afford to indulge in this weakness, for I always responded to the summons."

Mrs. Roosevelt certainly had learned to understand and accept people as they are.

At Val-Kill Cottage late one afternoon at the end of January, Mrs. Roosevelt tapped at the open door of my room where I was seated at the desk writing.

"William, I'm going to put some flowers on Franklin's grave—it's his birthday, you know—and I thought you might like to come with me and perhaps say a silent prayer."

I arose and followed Mrs. Roosevelt down to the flower room off the kitchen. It was like a pantry, equipped with metal sinks and a large variety of glass and pottery vases, jugs, and jars that were kept at the ready on the shelves. In season, all the rooms in the cottage, including occupied guest rooms, were bright with flowers. This particular afternoon, a bouquet of about two dozen assorted flowers, still wrapped in the florist's paper they had been delivered in, sat in water in a pail.

Mrs. Roosevelt was wearing FDR's tweed coat from his Harvard days, which was my signal to take my overcoat from the hall closet when we passed it. Mrs. Roosevelt dried off the bottom of the bouquet with a towel lying by the sink, and we set off to the car.

No one was at the gravesite in the Rose Garden, but three floral wreaths on stands had been placed near the flag. A light snow covered the ground.

Mrs. Roosevelt went to the ivy-covered grave, stood silently for a few moments, head bowed, and then kneeled, using the long skirt of the coat to protect her right knee. She placed the bouquet next to her and unwrapped it, distributing the flowers over the paper. I watched to see what she would do next. She took the first flower and placed it horizontally atop the ivy, threading the stem carefully through the leaves so that when she was finished only the blossom showed. Each flower was then selected in its turn and similarly woven into the emerging pattern. She herself moved three or four times in order to decorate the entire grave. There was no sound as she carried out what was clearly an absorbing ritual. The silence encompassed the devoted movements as the vibrant colors of the flowers spoke the language of the heart.

⚜

In addition to recounting her own memories of the President, Mrs. Roosevelt introduced William Turner Levy to a number of Franklin Roosevelt's relatives and friends so that he could discuss with them the nature of President Roosevelt's religious convictions. One of FDR's favorite relatives was his cousin, the dramatic Laura Delano.

Another source of information was David Gray, Mrs. Roosevelt's uncle by marriage. From Washington, Supreme Court Justice William O. Douglas wrote of the contrast between Roosevelt's belief in human equality and Churchill's disdain for the peoples of Asia. Bernard M. Baruch, the financier who held influential positions in several Democratic administrations, spoke up for the President's formidable mother Sara Delano Roosevelt, even though "You'll hear a great deal to the contrary." Other informants were New Dealers Henry A. Wallace, FDR's secretary of agriculture and later vice president; and Anna Rosenberg, who held various positions under Roosevelt, and later under President Truman.

⚜

To HELP IN MY RESEARCH on her husband's religious convictions, Mrs. Roosevelt made it possible for me to meet Miss Laura Delano, the President's cousin and a great favorite of his. Mrs. Roosevelt knew that Miss Delano would be a valuable source of intimate detail about Franklin's attitudes.

"I know you'll like Polly," Mrs. Roosevelt told me. "Franklin loved to have her around—she is so *original*, entertaining, and, of course, she was absolutely devoted to

Laura Delano, the president's cousin, was a great favorite of his and Mrs. R. A truly original and entertaining person, I was charmed and intrigued by her from the first meeting. *(Courtesy of the Franklin D. Roosevelt Library)*

him. He could relax with her. She would never badger him or argue with him as I would! I can appreciate now the pleasure he found, especially in the last year or so of his life, in being with Polly and Margaret Suckley, another cousin, whom you met when she was working on the photograph collection at the Hyde Park Library." She added, feelingly, "Franklin was more tired than any of us knew."

Mrs. Roosevelt said, "I will have to take you to Polly's for dinner sometime when she's at her house in Rhinebeck. The portions are small, but the courses are endless. The food is exquisitely prepared and served. I just find that it takes too long to eat such a meal—and somehow you feel an obligation to concentrate on the eating!"

It was arranged that Miss Delano would see me in her Sutton Place town house in New York. Her cousin, Frederick Delano Adams, director of the Morgan Library in New York, escorted me there and effected the introduction.

A maid in a crisp black-and-white uniform with a white cap led us to the living room, which opened out onto a private park, overlooking the East River and shared by the owners of the small houses that comprise the most exclusive block of private dwellings in the world's richest city.

It was a mild, clear day, and I was grateful that we had a few minutes to admire the East River in the background and the magnificent flowering magnolia tree in the foreground before Miss Delano entered.

Miss Delano walked briskly into the room and we turned to greet her. She was petite, but charged with nervous energy. On this occasion she was wearing a handsomely tailored red suit and red shoes, her hair was dark purple, her diamond rings and brooch were of staggering impressiveness. I thought at once how well the jewels suited her dramatic appearance, and could not imagine them suiting anyone else. She wore them with unconscious elegance, reminding me of Woodrow Wilson's famous remark to the widowed Mrs. Galt, who became his second wife: "You are the only woman I know who can wear an orchid. Most orchids wear the women!" Miss Delano greeted us jauntily. I was charmed and intrigued by her.

The oval living room walls were done in antique gold leaf and exotic painted birds and insects in exquisite shades flew from branch to branch of painted trees in this glorious room, part French in its feeling, part Asian. Strategically placed between the richly upholstered sofas and deep armchairs were tables bearing objets d'art: ivory on one table, jade on another, crystal on another, and one displaying nothing but small gold and silver boxes.

Another maid in a uniform identical to the first brought in a tray with ice and glasses and set it before Miss Delano, who industriously presided over a table with still more bottles set into its compartments.

"Would you like an old-fashioned, one of the President's favorite drinks?" she asked.

"I would indeed," I told her.

The potation was very strong and delightfully fragrant with its garnish of fruit cut to perfection. When I acknowledged its superiority to any old-fashioned I had ever tasted, Mr. Adams informed me that Polly's drinks were all superb.

"I think it's because I use sugar syrup," Miss Delano volunteered with bewitching mock modesty.

I was glad that I had brought my small leather notebook and gold pencil—nothing else would have suited that room. Miss Delano was generous with her memories, even though some of them moved her to tears. She told me things I would not have thought to ask; she shared with us her great love for the man she spoke of, and I was grateful, for I knew that it was not something she would have done except at the request of Mrs. Roosevelt.

My pencil rushed across the small pages, not wanting to miss a word or an inflection. Beyond interesting facts, I was also learning living details. Sometimes she was seeing him in her mind's eye. "I always think of him together with the wonderful smell of bay rum! In the morning, he would sweat so while dressing—it was such an effort—his shirt would be wet, beads of sweat would cover his face. Before breakfast, he'd kiss me, and . . ." (here her voice became scarcely audible) "in mock disapproval, I'd wipe off the sweat he'd left on my face. Then he'd throw back his head and laugh."

Looking down at her red shoes, she recalled, "He'd often say, 'Wear your red shoes, Polly!' and I would—to please him. I don't know what anyone thought, but I wore them to his funeral. For him."

Miss Delano told me of FDR's disdain for creature comforts. "I have never known a simpler man in my life." She tried to convey her loss: "He was tremendous! Gay!"

I thought of Yeats's triumphant line about the resilience of the ancient Chinese sages: "Their eyes . . . are gay."

ONE EVENING when Miss Delano was joining us for dinner, Mrs. Roosevelt forewarned me that she was bringing a newly acquired Pekinese, for which she had paid ten thousand dollars!

"I just felt you'd like to be sure you said something appropriate about the little treasure, and should he get under foot, take care not to step on the poor fellow!"

Mrs. Roosevelt was vastly amused anticipating her second "guest" of the evening.

The dog was a beautiful creature, a dark lustrous color with fabulous velvety fur, and possessed of a sweet disposition. When Mrs. Roosevelt and I were speaking of him privately over some late-night fruit and cookies, I made some disapproving comment about the outrageous price.

"The wealthy are rarely careless with money," she replied. "Laura is very canny, and you know her connection with the Westminster Dog Show. This newly acquired Pekinese will be available for stud at five hundred dollars! In no time she will have turned a handsome profit."

Another lesson from Mrs. Roosevelt. . . .

A CHARMING REMINISCENCE of FDR came to me from Charles Curnan, a member of a family long-employed by the Roosevelts, who had become Mrs. Roosevelt's chauffeur.

On a visit when I was doing research work at Hyde Park, "Tubby" most agreeably drove me back and forth to the library. I liked him at once. He asked that I call him "Tubby." He was stout, good-natured, sensible, and obviously dedicated to Mrs. Roosevelt. I judged him to be about 35, four years older than myself. I always sat up front with Tubby and we learned facts about each other. I was amused when he told me, with a laugh, that when he was in school he had to work hard on his studies because he had to show his report card to FDR. "He was mighty stern if it wasn't good," said Tubby, chuckling in remembrance. "Imagine having to show your report card to the President of the United States!"

One evening, shortly before cocktails, Mrs. Roosevelt came to my room. "I've asked Laura Delano for dinner. I knew you'd like that," she said, and I smiled in agreement.

Mrs. Roosevelt went on, "I know that she will like seeing you again. Now don't be shocked when she arrives. She could have green hair. The last time she came for dinner, her gown was absolutely diaphanous." We both laughed in anticipation of the company of FDR's extraordinary cousin Polly.

Miss Delano arrived in a beautiful black chiffon gown, which was the perfect foil for her multitude of dazzling diamonds, golden Arabian Nights slippers that curled up at the toe, and extra-long ivory cigarette holder. As we enjoyed our drinks, which it was my pleasure to make, we each talked about our day's activities. Anne Roosevelt was there with her son Haven, also Franklin Jr.'s wife, Sue, and their son Christopher, and Marie Morgan. I produced an editorial that FDR had written as editor-in-chief of the Harvard *Crimson*, in which he complained about the perfunctory conduct of the chapel services. I had discovered it that afternoon and was delighted with my find.

At our urging, Miss Delano began to tell us about her day. "I really haven't done a thing worth recounting," she told us loftily, poking the air with her cigarette in its long holder. "Except, well . . . this morning on my way from the kennels—I am a dog fancier, you know" (this was directed at me) "—I noticed this struggling rat who had gotten his leg about halfway out of a trap. I called several times, but the groom didn't hear me—no one did—so there was only one thing to do. I picked up a brick that was lying nearby and bashed the ugly fellow with all my might. I got blood all over myself, my dress, my stockings, but at least he wasn't going to get at my puppies!" she concluded indignantly. I thought at once that I would never underestimate a Delano.

That night, before retiring, Mrs. Roosevelt and I had what was becoming our traditional private chat, the time in the Hyde Park day I most looked forward to. Because I was expressing indignation over hypocritical "religious" morality as opposed to "having in you that mind which is in Christ Jesus"—I recall citing the Dodson sisters in *The Mill on the Floss*, who revered as Christianity whatever was "customary and respectable"—Mrs. Roosevelt told me that Sara Delano Roosevelt had this side to her character, making it all the more remarkable that FDR could break free of her standards and find true Christian values on his own.

"Franklin—to illustrate what I mean—remained shocked by the fact that his mother, as head of the family, refused to allow Franklin's half-brother Rosy to marry his French mistress of many years after his wife, the former Helen Astor, had died. Rosy had, in Sara Roosevelt's opinion, been living in sin all those years, yet when he was free to make an 'honest woman' of this lady, and rectify his own behavior, she refused to grant permission. Franklin was appalled that Rosy was not to be allowed to do the right and honorable thing because, as he was told by his mother, '*She* is not of our class.' Social distinctions were more important to her than true morality."

ANOTHER PRECIOUS SOURCE of information about FDR was Mrs. Roosevelt's uncle by marriage, David Gray, who had been the American minister to Ireland during World War II; his wife, Maude, was Mrs. Roosevelt's mother's youngest sister. Mrs. Roosevelt had tried to make all these relationships clear to me, but since most had nicknames as well as their proper names, I had some difficulty keeping Aunt Tissie and Auntie Bye, Auntie Corinne and Aunt Maude and Aunt Pussie and the others clear in my mind.

David Gray (left), here with Mrs. R, Anne and John Roosevelt, and
their daughter, had known FDR well and was a precious source of
information in the research for my book about FDR's religious beliefs.
(Courtesy of the Franklin D. Roosevelt Library)

In September 1955, I received a long, detailed letter
from the Honorable David Gray. He wrote from Portland,
Maine, where he spent his summers, for he divided his
time between that rocky northern seacoast and his house
on Siesta Key in Sarasota, Florida. He wrote of certain
periods of FDR's life with rare authority. For example, he
and his wife spent a month with Sara Delano Roosevelt
in her New York house during the winter of 1921, following FDR's attack of polio. There were connecting doors
between her house and the adjoining house, which she had
given to her son and daughter-in-law as a wedding present.
David Gray was invited to spend several hours a day with

the bedridden patient, playing gin rummy and discussing FDR's plans for the future.

Over the years, the Grays had spent visits of several weeks' duration at both Hyde Park and the White House, the last such visit being in 1943.

David Gray also wrote that as an undergraduate in the 1890s, he had studied under William James at Harvard and had retained a lively interest in supernormal phenomena. This fact was reflected in the way he closed his letter: "You have set yourself an interesting and difficult task. I wish you the best of luck. At the least it will give you an exercise in invoking guidance and insight."

I replied with gratitude. David Gray then invited me to meet with him for a conversation on the subject early in October when, passing through New York on his way to Sarasota, he would be spending a few days at the Knicker-bocker Club.

The elegant confines of the Knickerbocker Club provided the perfect setting for our first meeting. I knew little about David Gray beyond his public service as minister to Ireland and the few family details Mrs. Roosevelt had shared with me. I did know, however, that he had written a number of sporting books in the British tradition, the best-known of which were *Gallops I* and *Gallops II*. "He is rather like an American Surtees, I'd say," said Mrs. Roosevelt, referring to the English novelist and editor.

I was shown to a private book-lined sitting room by an usher who assured me that Mr. Gray would be with me presently. And indeed he was. He entered spryly, with the help of a silver-handled malacca cane. He was short but handsome, with a ruddy complexion that set off his white hair, and he couldn't have weighed more than 115 pounds.

His voice was pleasantly British in its range—thin, but colored with ample resonance; his diction was superbly cultivated, showing an instinctive valuing of the niceties of the English language—scholarly but not pedantic. His observant eyes were filled with a sense of fun, and his movements were elegant but spare, with no unnecessary dissipation of energy. Altogether a very young eighty-five!

"How very nice that we could meet," he said. When we had settled comfortably into deep black leather armchairs with a round table of beautiful patina between us, bearing a round-based black-and-gold lamp of oriental design, Mr. Gray suggested that we have drinks. I requested a bourbon on the rocks; he rang and ordered a whiskey for himself, too.

He spoke easily and informatively about FDR's family and childhood background: "Sara once told me, 'He is all my children in one,' and that is something you will have to understand in dealing with the relationship between mother and son." He spoke at length of FDR's curiosity about different kinds of people, how he enjoyed patiently picking their brains—"a thing that has never appealed to me; Franklin had an endless capacity to tolerate bores!" He told me of FDR's experimental nature, how he would build boat models, but at once abandon the theory if it didn't work in practice. "He was never tied to theories, had no loyalty to a dud idea."

He related how "Franklin and Eleanor started out with the idea that all older people were wrong. Eleanor was always knee-deep in new approaches, always with complete integrity and out of goodness of heart. Gradually, they learned from some rash mistakes, and trusted people less completely. They themselves were totally guileless."

Mr. Gray told me of his Good Friday audience with Pope Pius XII after a Sistine Chapel noon service and of the deep impression FDR's genuineness in his letters had made on His Holiness, who was not accustomed to this kind of exchange with heads of state.

There was so much for me to learn that I was delighted when Mr. Gray suggested I return the following day "armed with questions."

At our second afternoon meeting, I appreciated my host even more. He was confidential, witty, and charming and expressed his pleasure in my company. I noted that again he wore a brilliantly colored, generously proportioned bow tie that flattered him with its jauntiness. As on the previous day, I took notes and had searching questions to ask. In reference to FDR's crippling attack of polio, Mr. Gray said that he "never saw anybody like him!" Mr. Gray explained, "He, who had so loved physical exercise and the outdoor life, was absolutely uncomplaining! He was willing to renounce political life without a backward glance. He didn't have a smidgen of self-pity, and threw off the pity of others, often violently, to put a stop to it. At that time, he wouldn't go out to dinner, saying, 'I'm tired of being passed about like an entree!'"

ONE EVENING BEFORE RETIRING, Mrs. Roosevelt asked that I help her hang, alongside the Turner watercolors, a framed letter of Turner's that I had brought as a gift for my hostess. We then sat down and she told me how pleased she was that my research was going well.

"I'm especially pleased," she said animatedly, "that Justice Douglas wrote you that story about Franklin's rebuke to Churchill!"

In reply to my questions about FDR's religious attitudes, Supreme Court Justice William O. Douglas had written, in part:

> One thing that kept coming back to me as I reflected on your letter was a conversation I had with him sometime during World War II. It touches upon your reference to his fundamental belief in man's responsibility to his fellow man. He had been talking about his numerous conversations with Churchill. Churchill, the aristocrat and empire builder, apparently looked down upon the peoples of Asia, particularly the Chinese. Roosevelt told me how Churchill relished calling the Chinese "Pigtails" in rather contemptuous terms. He went on to tell me of his efforts to educate Churchill as to how the Chinese were also people and important in the universal scheme of things. He had a basic feeling for the equality of man and felt, I think, that without recognition of that principle there would be endless troubles in the world.

It was a gratifying bit of evidence because it helped document the strong contrast between FDR's approach to many problems, especially in the postwar world, and Churchill's—and at the same time it underscored the totally different effect of the same religious background upon the two men.

Mrs. Roosevelt said, "Mr. Churchill, my husband felt, was not the man to lead Britain *after* the war. Many of the qualities—for instance, doggedness—that made him a great wartime leader disqualified him for statesmanship in a period of international cooperation. That was another reason why Franklin wanted to get the United Nations set up *before* the war was over. He had lived, of course, very close to Wilson's fight for the League and knew how quickly wartime partnerships can fall apart."

"And isn't it interesting," I interjected, "that Britain did turn away from Churchill once the war was won."

"Yes," she replied, "although from across the distance of an ocean it seemed to many an ungrateful act."

I asked Mrs. Roosevelt if she had heard that Churchill had said, "The trouble with America is that she has gone from barbarism to decadence without having passed through civilization." She hadn't, and said she was always dubious of attributed stories. "But Winston could be cruel," she admitted.

ALSO IN CONNECTION WITH the research for my book, I had a reply from Bernard M. Baruch, setting an afternoon time for me to come to his New York office and discuss FDR. "I shall be happy to help a City College man," was his longhand addition to the letter.

It was natural, therefore, that he spoke first of City College. "I had to be frugal in those days, carried my sandwich and apple for lunch in a paper bag and walked, rather than spend the five-cent fare to ride to school." He thought back on those distant days with a strong affection, as was evident in his remark that he would "always be grateful to City College, always try to help it in any way possible."

As I was admiring his good looks, his height and broad shoulders, his waggish, determinedly youthful stance at eighty-five, he pointed a finger at me and said, enthusiastically, "Did you know I graduated in 1889? Now, what is that—forty years before you were born?" He laughed in the exuberance of his vitality, having no visible defect except his deafness.

Mr. Baruch frequently visited the Bernard M. Baruch School of Business and Public Administration of City College, where I taught, and I knew that the students were impressed when he deserted the faculty areas and sat down in the cafeteria to chat with them. On one occasion, shortly after Winston Churchill had been his house guest for a week, a student of mine reported that he had asked him about the fabulous Englishman, hoping for an intimate glimpse of greatness. Baruch, with his hearing aid off and in his pocket, as it probably had been all the week of Churchill's visit, brushed the question aside, "That fellow just drank brandy all the time and mumbled and mumbled and mumbled!"

Mr. Baruch was wearing a heavyweight tweed suit, tailored to perfection, with a brilliant red silk tie. His eyeglasses were pince-nez and his watch chain was heavy. He was talkative and clearly happy with my visit. I had the distinct impression that he enjoyed being with someone younger. "You should know," he said, with a wide smile, alluding to my theological background, "that the first Baruch was a loyal friend to the prophet Jeremiah!"

I admitted that I did.

"My father," the financier and adviser to presidents then confided, "was a great man, greatly loved. He was the father of hydrotherapy in this country, and he saw to it that it was provided for the poor! Just think, he was born in 1840." Mr. Baruch was fascinated by numbers, I could see—dates as well as financial figures. "And," he added with great pride, "he was a surgeon in the Confederate Army!"

Bernard M. Baruch was a great admirer of Mrs. R. When I interviewed him about FDR, he confided to me, "Isn't Mrs. Roosevelt a
peach?" *(Courtesy of the Franklin D. Roosevelt Library)*

"I'm frankly surprised that Roosevelt was so religious
a man," he said, "but from what you've told me of the
research you've done, there is clear evidence of it. I mean
conventionally religious. He had a strong conscience, I know,
and no shred of prejudice of any kind was in him, but it's
Wilson I think of as religious. I've seen him in the White
House get down on his knees and pray. His father was a
clergyman, you know."

I discovered that Mr. Baruch had a strong feeling for
Sara Delano Roosevelt. "The weekend that the *Greer* was
sunk was Franklin's mother's birthday weekend, and he had
planned to go to Hyde Park to be with her. Now he felt

the crisis demanded his presence at his desk in Washington. 'Nonsense,' I told him, 'you're always by a telephone and you can do as much there as you can here. Take an old man's advice. You only have one mother.' Well, he went to Hyde Park. It was her last birthday. After her death, he thanked me for deciding him to go and be with her. 'I'll always be grateful to you for that,' he said to me.

"And I must tell you," Mr. Baruch went on, "that Mrs. James Roosevelt was a wonderful lady. You'll hear a great deal to the contrary. I remember in Hyde Park once Franklin and I were having drinks before dinner and perhaps delaying a bit too long over them. His mother entered his study and said, 'Franklin, you're having a bad influence on Mr. Baruch. Now come along as soon as you can!' She walked toward the door. Then, without turning around, she said, 'And don't you wink behind my back, Franklin!'—which is precisely what he had done. She was a good sport and Roosevelt loved her deeply."

Before I left, Mr. Baruch signed my copy of his book, *A Philosophy for Our Time*. He said he'd always be glad to help, if he could. He added, shifting his gears into the present and taking me by the arm as he walked me to the door, "Isn't Mrs. Roosevelt a peach?"

MY RESEARCH ON FDR's religion continued. Mrs. Roosevelt was interested in the priceless unique details I was being given by the President's friends and associates. She was pleased to know that the work was going forward so successfully.

One evening after dinner at our home, I had my first opportunity to report to Mrs. Roosevelt my pleasure in meeting William D. Hassett. It was clear that Mrs. Roosevelt liked and trusted Hassett, whom she called Bill, and was happy that I had had the privilege of spending a long winter morning with him. So was I.

At seventy-six, William Hassett was a former newspaperman, a Vermonter, a scholarly, humorous, and knowledgeable intimate of the President—and he was eager to help me! He had first invited me to be his guest in Northfield, Vermont, an invitation I, unfortunately, was not free at the time to accept, so we met in New York.

They shared a love of books, the older the better. Their bantering relationship was, for the wartime president, a blessed tincture of lightness in the years of workdays. FDR, whose home was a sanctuary, took Mr. Hassett with him to Hyde Park more than forty times, and regaled him with Hudson River valley and family lore. He told Mr. Hassett in great detail a story out of his boyhood, about an old Hyde Park couple, so poor and proud that one died of hunger and cold before their plight was known.

Mr. Hassett recognized that Roosevelt's values were soundly based, and that he was a man full of fun but devoid of vulgarity—"an aristocrat to his fingertips."

Former Vice President Henry A. Wallace wrote to me from his farm in South Salem, New York, to state that it was his undoubted judgment that Franklin Delano Roosevelt had a "very deep and unwavering faith in God." He saw it as no superficial piety, and reminded me that he was conscientious in having his cabinet and close relatives attend Saint John's Episcopal Church with him on Lafayette Square, close to the White House, at the time of inaugurations and other important occasions. "Suffice it to say that he thought that justice was written into the eternal order of things and he was determined to do his part to see that justice triumphed."

Close to that time, I was granted the exceptional favor of a frank and illuminating conversation with FDR's physician, Howard Bruenn, from 1944 on, a heart specialist who was at the time a lieutenant commander in the Navy. He made it clear that he was seeing me and would withhold no details from me only because Mrs. Roosevelt had asked him to. He told me at once that he was indebted to her when, after the funeral, she had presented him with FDR's pocket watch as a token of esteem. The doctor told me, "So confident was the President that he would be spared to finish the work he was in, he never once asked about his state of health or the need for medication or the doctor's rules involving more sleep and rest." It was a unique experience for the doctor. "His mighty head, in death," Dr. Bruenn said, "was like our conception of a Hebrew prophet's in its augustness."

Also, I had Mrs. Roosevelt to thank for being invited to speak with Anna Marie Rosenberg, who held positions in the NRA, the Social Security Administration, and the War Manpower Commission, as well as serving under President Truman as assistant secretary of defense.

We met at her Madison Avenue office in New York, and we liked each other at once. The diminutive, obviously dedicated woman, who came to the United States in 1912 from Budapest, shared her memories and unabashedly shed tears eleven years after FDR's death, saying, "I grew old the day he died." She recalled that this man, who carried a world's burden, had a laugh that could be heard three rooms away. I commented that I could not begin to imagine the two Roosevelts together in a single room, and she agreed that it was an overwhelming experience. "But," she added thoughtfully, shyly, "if a choice needed to be made, you have the best of it with Mrs. Roosevelt."

It was not a confession I could share with the recipient of so supreme a compliment. I simply made brief, but grateful mention of these illustrious people that evening, for Mrs. Roosevelt had clearly made exceptional requests to them because of what she considered to be the importance of my project.

Chapter 11

Always a Democrat

ELEANOR ROOSEVELT REMAINED, *after her husband's death, the liberal figurehead of the Democratic Party. But she was a great deal more than a figurehead; she was a perceptive and influential participant in national politics. She, whose upbringing had been that of a sheltered patrician, who had avoided public speaking until Franklin's illness forced her to assume an active role, had learned over the years to play the game of politics, and to play it well. She found that she enjoyed it; she became, in fact, a consummate politician, a shrewd observer of the national scene, and an indispensable partner to the President during her years as First Lady.*

As the living symbol of liberalism in the Democratic Party, Mrs. Roosevelt had some very definite ideas about the party's policies and leadership. It was natural that she would often be asked to run for office, but she was adamant about her wish to remain independent.

࿇

MRS. ROOSEVELT WAS ASKED more than once to run for the office of United States Senator from the State of New

York. Everyone, including herself, agreed she would be a shoo-in. But she steadfastly refused to make herself a political figure. She was fierce in the determination to keep her independence. She knew that a good politician needed to make compromises and, upon occasion, hew to the party position, even if it was one he or she had unsuccessfully fought to have changed or modified.

Mrs. Roosevelt said, "I may be wrong, but I think any influence I may have stems from the fact that I speak only for myself."

All arguments for the good she could accomplish in the thick of the fray and for the role that she would play in forwarding the status of women in public office fell on deaf ears.

Mrs. Roosevelt told me that the brilliant and tenacious Louis Howe, who contributed so effectively during FDR's years as governor of New York to setting the political stage that resulted in FDR's nomination for the presidency in 1932, was musing aloud one day during that first term in the White House that eventually FDR might decide not to run again. He said, "The way must be paved, we must look to the future for a perfect candidate for the Democratic Party. . . . Ah, . . . a woman!"

"He looked me right in the eye," said Mrs. Roosevelt. "I fled. He just might have done it, you know! He had the uncanny gifts of a president maker! Being a small, gnome-like man, racked with illnesses, he loved the exercise of a power he could never use to his own advantage." She laughed as she recalled that harrowing moment. "I quite literally *fled!*"

Eleanor Roosevelt believed that Adlai E. Stevenson had the true ability to lead the Democratic Party in the postwar period; however, he was defeated in the Eisenhower landslide of 1952. The Democrats would turn to him again in 1956. But, once again, he was defeated by Eisenhower.

§◊§

IT WAS NOMINATING NIGHT, 1956, at the Democratic National Convention in Chicago. Mrs. Roosevelt had been there earlier in the day spearheading the nomination of Adlai E. Stevenson. *Life* magazine's cover the following week would show two beaming Democrats—Adlai E. Stevenson and Eleanor Roosevelt, who was proudly wearing her "Adlai" campaign button for all to see!

In order to participate in Mrs. Roosevelt's appearance at the convention, I bought my first television set, a concession on my part that she fully appreciated. Late that afternoon on August 16, I received a telephone call from Mrs. Roosevelt's secretary, Maureen Corr. She said, "Dr. Levy! Wasn't she just wonderful!" I heartily agreed. Miss Corr continued: "Mrs. Roosevelt just telephoned. She's flying back to New York from Chicago and would like you to dine alone here with her this evening and watch the nomination." I was overwhelmed. She was stepping out of this uproarious national spotlight into absolute privacy.

I arrived shortly before Mrs. Roosevelt and made myself a martini. Irene, the cook, had set up a card table so that we could dine before the television set. The scene was warmly inviting.

We had a very different kind of dinner, one at which I recorded the votes, state by state, as we watched and dined and exchanged pleasantries. Irene served us smoked

Mrs. R with Adlai E. Stevenson at Hyde Park. They were certainly a mutual admiration society. *(Courtesy of William Turner Levy)*

salmon, accompanied, as always, by the expertly cheese-cloth-wrapped lemon wedges. The steak was just what we wanted, whether we'd known it in advance or not, and I had earlier selected the Pouilly-Fuissé and, for the main course, an Alox-Corton. Irene's always fabulous apple stru-del with its paper-thin envelope of dough was delivered still warm for dessert.

At exactly 10:56 P.M., Governor Stevenson was nomi-nated with the vote of 686 to 5!

Close to midnight, while I was savoring a brandy and Mrs. Roosevelt was indulging in a rare, celebratory crème de menthe, Governor Stevenson telephoned.

Mrs. Roosevelt said to him, "Congratulations, Adlai! I couldn't be happier for you and for us. Will Levy and I have been glued to the set and enjoyed a quiet dinner

together . . . yes, I'll tell him. And thank you for *calling*!"
Mrs. Roosevelt turned to me and said, "Adlai thanks you
for your work on his Writer's Committee."

Before leaving, I asked Mrs. Roosevelt to sign our tally
sheet, which I meant to keep as a souvenir of a gala
evening.

"Franklin would have asked the same thing!" she said
smiling, as she complied. "He had a keen sense of history."

❧

*Four years later, in the days before the Democratic convention of
1960, potential candidates sought out Mrs. Roosevelt in hopes of
winning her endorsement. She was perfectly aware of how
politicians operated, as William Turner Levy had already had
occasion to observe in 1955 when her Republican son, John, was
flattered by a call from Vice President Richard Nixon. In the
case of Lyndon B. Johnson she provided William Turner Levy
with yet another short lesson in discernment.*

❧

MRS. ROOSEVELT'S REPUBLICAN SON, John Roosevelt, sat
on an anti-discrimination committee chaired by Vice President Nixon. One morning in 1955 he walked from his
nearby home across the lawns to Val-Kill Cottage. A small
group of family and friends had recently finished breakfast.
I was already at the library doing research.

John Roosevelt brought the news that President Eisenhower had suffered a coronary but that it was not a serious
attack.

That evening, Mrs. Roosevelt and her guests were
invited to dine with John and his wife, Anne, at their home.
During the course of dinner, John, in his always boyish but

self-important way, related that "Dick Nixon telephoned to tell me about the president's heart attack. He was very brief, said he had hundreds of calls to make." John cleared his throat to emphasize, "Wasn't that nice of him? He said that the news of it would not be released for several hours, but he wanted me to know in advance that it was not a serious attack. I guess he didn't want me to worry." John felt very much an insider.

Before turning in that night, I commented to Mrs. Roosevelt on the news. "That was thoughtful of Nixon, wasn't it?"

Mrs. Roosevelt's quizzical look at me conveyed that I was unbelievably naïve. "John didn't get it either," she said. "The giveaway was that he was in a great rush because he had *hundreds* of calls to make."

I must have retained my blank expression.

Mrs. Roosevelt explained to me, "Nixon was calling everyone who might be politically important to him in the future. The stock market would fall heavily when the news was released. These people had the inside information that in a few days the doctors would issue reassuring statements of the president's recovery. They would buy in the stock market where prices had tumbled, knowing that they were in to make truly big profits when the good news came out and prices went up. And they would always be indebted to Nixon for their windfall."

MRS. ROOSEVELT PROVIDED ME with exceptional opportunities to share a relaxed time over a meal with people at the highest level of achievement. Adlai E. Stevenson, despite a marked shyness, was brilliantly communicative. President

Truman was warmly interesting in himself and warmly interested in you. A searching conversation between Mrs. Roosevelt and the great American labor union leader Walter Reuther ranged creatively over fresh possibilities for a fuller life open to the worker of the future thanks to automation and diminished working hours. Lyndon B. Johnson had charm. He told me I represented in one man the two vocations he most honored, the clergyman and the teacher.

Johnson and I talked for hours before he planted a tree to honor FDR and departed. Thinking to make notes of this meeting, as was my custom, I was astonished to find that I couldn't remember a single thing he had said. Sharing this fact with Mrs. Roosevelt when we were alone having cheese and crackers before retiring, I discovered she was in agreement.

"Lyndon came a-courtin'" was her sing-song verdict. "He wants to be president, but try as I did, I couldn't learn about a single program he had formulated." She repeated herself, "Lyndon wants to be president." Then she added with approving frankness, "Franklin was *willing* to become president because only as president could he introduce legislation that he felt was essential to end the Depression!"

※

John F. Kennedy was another contender for the Democratic nomination in 1960; however, Mrs. Roosevelt continued to believe in Adlai E. Stevenson as the Democrat who most embodied the liberal values she cherished, and she hoped that Stevenson would make a final bid for the presidency. Kennedy, by contrast, struck her as an equivocator who could not be counted on to stand up for principle. He had failed to speak out against Senator McCarthy, a grievous fault in her mind. He was immature. He was too much under the influence of his father, a man reputedly willing to spend millions to make his son president.

William Turner Levy was instrumental in paving the way for a crucial meeting between Mrs. Roosevelt and John F. Kennedy. At lunch in Hyde Park, the two Democratic leaders took one another's measure and began the slow move toward reconciliation. By the next spring Kennedy, now President, took advantage of their rapprochement to ask Mrs. Roosevelt for help.

৪৯৪

I MET SENATOR JOHN F. KENNEDY by introducing myself to him. He was in front of Tiffany's on the corner of Fifth Avenue and 57th Street waiting for the light to turn so that he might cross the street. I identified myself, not leaving out my friendship with Mrs. Roosevelt, while we shook hands for the first time and smiled broadly. No one was easier to meet.

As I later learned from experience was a focus of mind with him, he immediately set out to learn something useful to himself. "Why doesn't Mrs. Roosevelt like me?" he asked. So blunt a question elicited a straightforward answer, as he had expected. "Mrs. Roosevelt has no reason to dislike you, Senator, she simply doesn't admire you."

"Is it because she feels my stand against Senator McCarthy wasn't strong enough?" he asked, rather as if, even if true, that was no longer an issue.

"That's certainly true," I replied, "but in her mind it was symptomatic of a failure to stand and be counted when the chips were down."

With irritation in his tone, he pondered, "I suppose I'll never be able to put that behind me."

"Well, Senator, Mrs. Roosevelt is far too intelligent to imagine that a person can't change. The present is not necessarily the captive of the past. If I were you, sir, I'd sit down with her, for certainly you both have more in common than could possibly divide you. You both want a Democrat in the White House."

The traffic lights had changed several times. The Senator concentrated on me, and so was not distracted by other admiring pedestrians. This, too, I was to discover by experience was a technique he had perfected as a way of defending his privacy, like the way he would back you into a corner of a room to cut off everyone else present, giving them only his back. He asked if I ever came to Washington. I told him that I went down once a year, visited the National Gallery of Art, and at night made pilgrimage to the Lincoln and Jefferson memorials.

"At night! So do I! No crowds then, a chance to have their illuminated presence to yourself. So beautiful, so quiet. Telephone my secretary at the Senate Office Building when next you are planning to come down, and she'll set up an appointment."

He shook my hand, thanked me, and strode briskly across Fifth Avenue. He was more youthful than I had been prepared for.

Of course, I made an early opportunity to accept that invitation, taking along my mother, who was particularly fond of the capital.

True to his word, we had a leisurely and fascinating visit with him in his office. His sensitivity was surely the most innate of his virtues, so, in courtesy and in order to prolong his good-bye, he escorted my mother and me from the quiet of his office out into the pushing clamor of a public corridor. I protested his kindness. He stopped where he stood, took us both by our arms, and said, with revealing earnestness, "It's five twenty-five now. I've been here since early morning. I'll probably be here until after seven—and you're the only two persons who've been here today who haven't wanted something."

Senator Kennedy came to Hyde Park to address a rally commemorating the twenty-fifth anniversary of the creation of Social Security. Mrs. Roosevelt invited him and his party, which included Pierre Salinger, to lunch at Val-Kill Cottage. Marge set up a bridge table in the living room for the senator and his hostess to lunch privately. Mrs. Roosevelt asked my mother to be hostess at the dining room table for the other guests.

Almost immediately after lunch, the senator left. I had known that his time would be limited and had prepared a one-page memorandum to give him, presenting some ideas I hoped might be helpful. He astonished me by taking it from the envelope and reading it in a matter of seconds, and then showing one statement to Mrs. Roosevelt and asking if she agreed that this might be the case. She read it and said that on that subject I was an expert. He thanked me and, returning the sheet to its envelope, put it in his breast pocket. Speaking once of FDR, Mrs. Roosevelt had taught me that any communication had to fit on one page, as time was a busy leader's most valuable commodity. She now added that the senator had indeed read the memorandum thoroughly, for she knew he'd recently completed a speed-reading course in anticipation of the mountains of paperwork in the White House.

When John F. Kennedy came to Val-Kill during his campaign
for the presidency, I gave him a memorandum I had prepared.
Later, he asked his private secretary, Evelyn Lincoln, to tell me
that this is the only photograph in existence signed by both
him and Eleanor Roosevelt. *(Courtesy of William Turner Levy)*

That afternoon, at the request of John and Anne
Roosevelt, I held the funeral service for their thirteen-
year-old daughter, Sally, who had been killed when she was
thrown from a horse a few days earlier. Sally had liked me,
and Mrs. Roosevelt told me that John and Anne felt especially comforted to be able to call on me at this terrible

moment. That evening, I expressed to Mrs. Roosevelt my sadness that at her age she should have to suffer the loss of a grandchild. She told me, frankly, that because she *was* older, she felt the grief less intensely. It was her youngest son and his wife for whom her heart was sore.

She changed the subject. "Well, I have met Mr. Kennedy," she confided, with an intonation carrying little enthusiasm. In the pause that followed she adjusted the position of the leather-banded man's watch on her left wrist and then the ring on the small finger of the same hand. It was a characteristic gesture indulged in when she was pensive.

"He was a changed man when he emerged from that luncheon meeting," I said. "It was a physical difference, partly a chastened expression and partly his way of looking at you, a newfound respect, even awe, an emotion with which I'm sure he's not familiar. I was not surprised, although I could not have anticipated it. He simply did not know you, and now he did. What *did* you say to him?"

"My response to his question about my lukewarm support centered on my judgment that strong convictions and the courage to act on them were the prerequisites for command leadership. I followed that with his less than admirable voting record in the Senate and my refusal to accept an absence, convenient or otherwise, as an excuse for not being on record. I told him that he needed to show vigorous and enthusiastic support for the basic tenets of the Democratic Party."

"Is that all?" I interjected.

"Well, not quite, but that was the gist of it. After all, *he* sought this meeting and I saw no reason to pull any punches," Mrs. Roosevelt said, a naughty twinkle in her eyes. "He's very young in many ways, but we'll see if he really means to learn."

Mrs. Roosevelt went on: "He did ask for my advice. He said that he had difficulty in dealing with Black leaders and in speaking to Black groups. What was he doing wrong? I told him that victims of prejudice grow antennae of incredible sensitivity, even oversensitivity. They cannot be fooled or sweet-talked. They will identify exactly what you feel and where you stand in relation to them. Then I advised him that since he was uncomfortable in those situations because he was not absolutely genuine in his response to these people, he should keep away from them, avoid all contact insofar as possible, be represented by others—or remake himself!"

Mrs. Roosevelt confided emphatically, "I told Mr. Kennedy that I would follow his campaign closely and that I would support him step-by-step as he proved his commitment to the Democratic programs step-by-step. At this time I could not blanketly support him. Then, to encourage him, I promised that I looked forward to the time when I *could* endorse him wholeheartedly. 'I will even campaign actively,' I added, 'making appearances and speeches in areas where you and your people think I could make a difference.' This appeared to please him immensely."

No wonder he looked to be a changed man. He must have been stunned by her political acumen. Mrs. Roosevelt was not the matriarchial figurehead of the Democratic Party he had mistakenly imagined. He discovered that she was not one more supporter to be won by promises or charm. She had exacted from him her price—that he prove himself a leader of presidential status, capable of being elected by the American people. Only then would he earn the reward of her influential name.

Fittingly, after Mrs. Roosevelt's death, President Kennedy said, "Truly, Eleanor Roosevelt was the imperishable conscience of the world."

છ૭છ

Eleanor Roosevelt saw promise in John F. Kennedy's inaugural address. "I have re-read your words several times," she wrote him, "and I am filled with thankfulness. May we all respond to your leadership and make your task easier."

છ૭છ

THE TRACES OF the great Washington snowfall on Inauguration Day 1961 were still visible eight days later when President Kennedy was faced with a major foreign policy inheritance from the Eisenhower administration, which had decided to arm and drill Cuban exiles in Guatemala in preparation for a possible invasion of Castro's Cuba and to install a committee of Cuban politicians, now in Florida under American auspices, on Cuban soil as a provisional government. This project had been decided upon some nine months earlier, and many factors required that it be put into effect without delay. The CIA, the Joint Chiefs of Staff, and the secretary of state all approved. The new president was surrounded by advisers whose judgment he had not tested personally. The eight hundred exiles (which later grew to fourteen hundred men) were determined to go. There was pressure from Guatemala to get them out of the country; if the project were called off, the men would be brought to the United States and would be disgruntled, revealing their "betrayal." If all this was not enough, the rainy season was almost upon the area to thwart military movement, and jet airplanes with Cuban pilots trained in Czechoslovakia were about to be delivered to Castro from the Soviet Union.

The president approved. In mid-April, the so-called (because of the landing area selected) Bay of Pigs invasion was a humiliating fiasco for the new president, a major foreign policy defeat. The nation was in shock.

Ten days later, at the end of April, I was at breakfast alone with Mrs. Roosevelt at Val-Kill Cottage. Her back was to the dining room window, the sun was streaming in, warming the room and lighting the silver pieces on the sideboard to an almost golden glow.

Mrs. Roosevelt was pouring our tea, straining it through the ornate silver strainer that had belonged to her grandmother Hall. She fed the bread, as was her custom, into the toaster at her side, and when it popped up, she gingerly extracted the hot toast with her fingers and passed me a slice on which I spread sweet butter and some homemade crab apple jelly. We cut the tops off our soft-boiled eggs and, having salted and peppered them, dug into the golden centers with the mother-of-pearl spoons.

We heard the telephone ring. Marge Entrup entered to say, "It's the White House, Mrs. Roosevelt."

Mrs. Roosevelt nodded and promptly picked up the extension telephone on the sideboard. "Yes, Mr. President?"

I stood up at once to give her privacy, but she frowned, shook her head, and indicated that I was to continue my breakfast.

"Not at all," she said into the phone.

She listened intently for some minutes, then replied, "Of course, I understand."

Pause. Then she said with a chuckle, "I'm somewhat used to that. I will do my best, Mr. President."

She hung up, reached for my teacup, poured for me, rang for Marge, and requested more hot water. Marge took the silver water jug, and Mrs. Roosevelt popped bread in the toaster, first asking, "White or whole wheat?"

Then she told me. "The president is deeply distressed over the fate of the free men we put on the Cuban beaches. It seems that Castro will only release the captives for twenty-odd million dollars and five hundred bulldozers. The United States government cannot engage in such ransom, but private citizens can. The president has asked me to head a 'Tractors for Freedom Committee' to raise from public contributions money to purchase tractors (for agriculture, you see, not bulldozers, which might be used militarily) and, as well, ambulances, for humanitarian purposes. Of course, I said I would do anything to help free them. He said that he would ask Walter Reuther [the American trade union leader and an important anticommunist liberal spokesman] to join the committee, as well, and Dr. Milton Eisenhower [the president of Johns Hopkins University and brother of the former president], the latter being a Republican who would create bipartisan support."

Mrs. Roosevelt paused to munch some toast and then continued. " 'You realize,' the president told me, 'that you will be bitterly attacked from some quarters.' I told him that I was somewhat used to that! Then he said, 'Mrs. Roosevelt, I will not be able to come to your defense. I must distance myself and the government far from your efforts. If asked, I know nothing about it. You are acting as a private citizen out of conscience. We have endangered these men and I cannot sleep if we do not rescue them. I know you have every reason to understand. I need your help, both personally and as your president.'"

In about three months the Tractors for Freedom Committee dissolved, bogged down by political controversy and Dr. Eisenhower's withdrawal under fire. Later, through private contributions of food and medical supplies, the rescue was effected.

A year later, during the nuclear missile crisis that arose from the Russians building missile bases in Cuba, President Kennedy confronted Khrushchev as peoples everywhere watched with bated breath. Mankind had its long-dreaded nuclear annihilation nightmare.

The president consulted, weighed tangibles and intangibles, and then knew exactly what to do. His triumph dazzled the world.

At that April breakfast, Mrs. Roosevelt's confidence in me allowed me to learn two never-failing practical lessons: all is not as it appears—and trust between individuals is beyond price.

Chapter 12

Friendship

FRIENDSHIPS ARE NOURISHED through conversations, through hospitality given and received, through spontaneous gifts and other mutual gestures of remembrance and affection. The friendship of William Turner Levy and Eleanor Roosevelt grew in all these ways. One measure of their deepening relationship was Mrs. Roosevelt's desire for greater informality in the names they used for each other.

༄༅

AN AIR MAIL LETTER with impressive orange stamps, dated August 23, 1955, and sent from the Peninsula Hotel in Hong Kong, read, "Thank you so much for your little note. I shall look forward to hearing from you in Bangkok and to seeing you when I get home." In longhand was added: "So far our trip has been most interesting."

This was the first time Mrs. Roosevelt addressed me as "William" and signed a letter, "Affectionately yours."

ONE SATURDAY AFTERNOON in autumn when I was doing research at Hyde Park, Mrs. Roosevelt drove over at five o'clock as arranged, to pick me up and bring me to Val-Kill Cottage to have a swim and dress for dinner.

Unexpectedly, Mrs. Roosevelt pulled over and parked under a huge sycamore tree just off the side road we usually traveled. She turned in the driver's seat to face me and said: "I would like you to call me Mrs. R, rather than Mrs. Roosevelt. I know you wouldn't be comfortable with 'Eleanor,' which only the family and two or three old friends use. But 'Mrs. Roosevelt' is too formal for us. You know, William, that the other evening when we were having one of our late-night discussions just before bedtime, you spoke to me for the first time as if I were your grandmother, not 'Mrs. Roosevelt.' I loved it! You got through the public persona and I was deeply touched. We all need to be accepted for ourselves, the person we are to ourselves and our few intimates. One can only hope that it will happen. It did. Do you understand?"

"Yes, Mrs. Roose . . . Mrs. R," I stumbled.

"Now, I have one more thing to say. Any home of mine is open to you at any time—whether in New York or here in Hyde Park, or any other I may acquire. You do not have to be invited to come. You may stay as long as you like, a day, a week, months. You may bring anyone you would like with you. This applies whether I'm in residence or not. I will tell the staff of this and they will welcome you and take care of you. In short, you have a second home. Use it whenever it will be good for you. It's nice to have a private refuge, a place of your own."

With that, Mrs. R turned, and drove us "home." I said nothing, nor, I am sure, was I expected to.

It was darkening into early evening. Seen through the windshield, the autumn colors were beautiful. The world was preternaturally beautiful. Tears of happiness blurred my vision.

&❧&

The two friends found that they shared common interests in literature, music, and the theater. They learned one another's tastes and enjoyed giving each other carefully chosen, though not necessarily lavish, gifts. Books were a favorite choice. On one memorable occasion William Turner Levy was the fortunate beneficiary of the gift of a Tashkent chieftain.

&❧&

MRS. ROOSEVELT WAS an *aficionada* of the theater. She delighted in few things more than an evening in which we put ourselves in the hands of actors. She had seen Bernhardt and Duse on stage; indeed, when she was a child, her Aunt Pussie had taken her to meet the great Italian actress. I, too, was fortunate to have seen many unforgettable performances: Richardson's Falstaff, Olivier's Oedipus and Shallow, Cornell's Cleopatra, Ethel Barrymore's Miss Moffat. It was a passion we shared. So were concerts. And films.

The first film Mrs. Roosevelt took me to was Kurosawa's *The Seven Samurai*. It was an invitational showing to benefit the International Rescue Committee, whose honorary chairman was Admiral Richard E. Byrd. That evening I met General William J. Donovan, Angier Biddle Duke, and Joshua Logan. It was a gala occasion.

On another occasion, Mrs. Roosevelt took me to a benefit dinner and concert for the American Hungarian Medical Association at the Plaza Hotel. The soloist I best remember was the violinist Joseph Szigeti. That year

Dimitri Mitropoulos conducted the Pension Fund Benefit Concert of the New York Philharmonic Orchestra and Renata Tebaldi was the soloist in an all-Verdi program.

I did not see Dore Schary's play about FDR's contraction of polio, *Sunrise at Campobello*, with Mrs. Roosevelt, though I was later to visit with both Mr. Schary and Ralph Bellamy, who portrayed FDR. Mrs. Roosevelt preferred to see it, but not herself be seen, sitting in the last row at the back of the theater. It was a fine play and was later made into a successful film. Naturally, I asked Mrs. Roosevelt her reaction to so intimate a subject on stage, including herself and her children and mother-in-law as principals. "I felt it was beautifully done and a moving experience, but I never felt for a minute that it was about us—I could not have felt more remote from the characters themselves." Her reaction was due to the passage of time.

Another night at the New York Philharmonic, Leonard Bernstein was conducting and Mischa Elman was soloist. Mrs. Roosevelt was particularly looking forward to Mendelssohn's Concerto for Violin and Orchestra in E minor. Earlier in the program, we had heard some "first performance in New York" and other new and experimental compositions. As was her wont, once the lights went down, my concert-going companion promptly went to sleep—a worthy protection even against trumpet and percussion. However, on the first note of the Mendelssohn, she was awake and all ears!

Over the years we saw many productions, major and minor, among them: *The Rivalry, Four Bags Full, Héloïse, Rhinoceros*, Tagore's *King of the Dark Chamber*, and one film that left us impressed, but perplexed, *The Seventh Seal*.

When we went to see *Becket*, Mrs. Roosevelt, assuming that I would like to meet and converse with Sir Laurence

Olivier, arranged for us to go backstage. It was a stimulating half hour over drinks with an incomparable actor who we discovered was also a shy and elegant man.

We always, or almost always, found much to share in our reactions once we got home. After seeing Archibald MacLeish's *JB*, a play based on the Book of Job, Mrs. Roosevelt and I stayed up until after one in the morning comparing the depth of the original with the shortcomings of the fascinating modern version. Perhaps, we concluded, some supreme works had best be left to speak for themselves. The intellectual passion of our observations was nicely tempered by a chocolate cake miraculously awaiting us!

In October 1962 we were to attend a performance of the Leningrad Philharmonic on its first American tour, but Mrs. Roosevelt called to say that she did not feel up to it. I went alone. I do not remember a single piece that was played that night.

FROM CHILDHOOD I knew the line, "I kiss your hand, Madame," from some long-forgotten song, but the act never became a reality for me until I met Mrs. Roosevelt.

When she took me to lunch at the United Nations dining room, our progress to the table was punctuated by an array of gentlemen, some exotically garbed, rising to kiss Madame Roosevelt's hand. It was a lovely sight.

A stark but strikingly dramatic new restaurant in New York, which unfortunately did not endure, was the site of a small dinner party given for Mrs. Roosevelt. A spare, aging gentleman in a gray flannel suit, possessed of a handsome head and face, bright, penetrating eyes, and a perfect nose, approached our table with catlike silence and grace. It was, I recognized, Max Ernst, the pioneer of surrealism, whom someone had called the gentlest of the giants of twentieth-century art.

I rose from my seat next to Mrs. Roosevelt and stood aside. She turned and smiled a delighted smile of recognition. He bowed, kissed her hand, and in the softest of voices, murmured, "Madame Roosevelt." The act was a symbolic accolade.

Backstage at *Becket*, Sir Laurence Olivier kissed Mrs. Roosevelt's hand both when we arrived and again as we departed, his entire body clothed in masculine grace.

When Mrs. Roosevelt and I attended a Philadelphia Orchestra concert conducted by Sir Malcolm Sargent, the English half of the concert included a work by Ralph Vaughan Williams. After the intermission, we heard a rewarding performance of Sibelius's Second Symphony.

I cannot remember why Mrs. Roosevelt was invited backstage, but it was a glorious sight to see the impeccable Sir Malcolm, looking incredibly youthful and sporting the never-absent white carnation in his buttonhole, come to attention, greet Mrs. Roosevelt, kiss her hand, and affably accept her introduction of myself.

Since I knew Vaughan Williams, I commented on the delightful rendition of *The Wasps*. Sir Malcolm told me he would convey my greeting when he saw Vaughan Williams the next week. I was so glad we had gone backstage.

The Dutch-born French painter Kees van Dongen, one of the leading fauvists after Matisse, and his wife, came to Val-Kill Cottage for lunch. Mrs. Roosevelt had asked me to come because the four of us spoke French. A stout, humorous man in his eighties, he was clearly enjoying life. I did not know his work well, but Mrs. Roosevelt had reminded me of his particularly notable portrait of Anatole

France done about 1917. As he did not talk about himself, that was all I needed to know at that point.

He told us that his friend Pierre Bonnard, one of the greatest colorists of modern art, had no business sense at all. "I was present," he told us with great animation, "when a rich American patron of art visited his studio. The man chose two superb Bonnards, taking time to study them in the best light, and asked the price. Bonnard couldn't think what to ask. After an awkward pause, the American stated a generous figure. My friend at once replied, 'No, no, that is too much!' *Bonnard était fou.*" Mad, indeed.

As they were preparing to leave, I asked Mrs. Roosevelt in an aside if it would be all right to ask him for his autograph. "I think he would be pleased," she replied.

I produced a sheet of Val-Kill stationery and made my request. Mrs. Roosevelt was right—he was delighted. Taking a pen from his pocket he produced a simple drawing of a man's hat—and signed it.

"May I ask, M. van Dongen, why a hat?"

He burst out laughing, put on his own hat, raised it, smiled broadly, and said, "I say to you—*au revoir!*"

He then kissed his hostess's hand.

GIFTS SPEAK FOR US, and often the simpler, the better. A Scottish sweater from Mrs. Roosevelt still warms me, individual nut dishes from a trip to Russia often appear on my dinner table, an elegant neckerchief from Paris is worn on special occasions. New Year's telegrams, vibrant Easter lilies, and crates of comice pears are not forgotten.

Mrs. Roosevelt didn't require possessions, but she reveled in fine soaps, the first lilacs of the season, candied Australian apricots, a few autumn leaves mailed from

Vermont—not to mention salt water taffy from Atlantic City and a tiny pot of shamrocks from Ireland on Saint Patrick's Day.

Books, books above all! I gave her my recently published *William Barnes: The Man and the Poems* and sent books by my friends: Mark Van Doren, Reinhold Niebuhr, Bishop James A. Pike, T. S. Eliot. It was exciting introducing her to Maurice Reckitt's *Prospect for Christendom*, the work of Denis de Rougemont, Simone Weil, Rampa's *The Third Eye: Autobiography of a Tibetan Lama*. Not to mention each Walt Kelly *Pogo* book as it came out, once the very first one converted her to an interest in the denizens of Okefenokee Swamp. In 1959, each of us, in the wild attempt to be first, simultaneously gifted each other with *Ten Ever-Lovin' Blue-Eyed Years with Pogo!*

Inscribed copies of all of Mrs. Roosevelt's own books came my way, and she introduced me to Dinah Maria Mulock's landmark nineteenth-century English novel *John Halifax, Gentlemen*, whose hero, one of nature's noblemen and a forerunner of Adam Bede and Enoch Arden, she describes as the possessor of that great human quality "dependableness."

I must name a few others. Lillian Smith's *The Journey*, a book of memoirs and experiences: "It never occurred to me that when something happens to you, *you* in turn happen to it. It is *you* who make the next move, *you* who decide what meaning the experience is going to have for you." *One Hour*, also by Lillian Smith, a novel which, Mrs. Roosevelt said in her inscription, she hoped I would find an experience. The central character is an Episcopal priest struggling to be worthy of his vocation: "They go to church, but the god they worship is the image of themselves." Tangentially, the book contains references to many with whom I was familiar, a fact that she didn't tell me, but let me discover for myself: Niebuhr, Eliot, Jeffers, Vaughan Williams, de Rougement.

In Puerto Rico, Mrs. Roosevelt read Ruth Suckow's subtle novel of doing what one could to help right a wrong, *The John Wood Case*. The high school boy at the heart of the story believed that the name Philip suited him. "He had never read Sir Philip Sidney's sonnets . . . but knew only that Sir Philip gave his cup of water to his dying enemy." It, too, was an experience for me.

Another gift from Mrs. Roosevelt, the elaborate catalog to a philosophical art exhibition entitled *The Heroic Encounter*, deals with the spiritual wisdom that evil is internal and must be subdued first in the self. The "hero" symbolizes reason, intelligence, refinement of spirit, a David as opposed to Goliath. The volume is rich in quotations. Pablo Picasso: "What do you think an artist is? A fool, who, if he is a painter, has only eyes, if he is a musician, only ears, if he is a poet, only a lyre for all the chords of the heart, or even if he is a boxer, only muscles? On the contrary, he is . . . always wide-awake in the face of the heart-rending bitter or sweet events of the world and wholly fashioning himself according to their image. . . . No, painting is not made to decorate houses. It is a weapon of offensive and defensive war against the enemy." St. John Perse: "And singing to us the honor of living, ah! Singing to us and singing to us from the very summit of peril."

I had given Mrs. Roosevelt a carved wooden angel and blessed it for her. She placed it over her bed in New York, so I soon found another for her bed at Hyde Park.

On a trip to Europe, she wrote from Paris, "You would have been delighted with the Easter Service we attended in old Jerusalem and I only wish you could have been with us."

From London she brought me a copy of the New Testament designed by Hans Mardersteig, the text printed in Italy, the illustrations in France, and the cloth binding in Holland. The illustrations are from the *Très Riches Heures* of the duc de Berry (1340–1416) and executed for him by Paul de Limbourg and his brothers on the finest vellum, creating landscapes and figures in the most delicate colors and luminous blue skies of brilliance and depth, using precious lapis-lazuli as the source. *The Announcement to the Shepherds* is startling, but the sheep and the dog are indifferent! *Cure of the Possessed Boy* takes place in an elaborately formal setting, but the stark realism breaks through. In *Ego Sum—the Betrayal*, the world is darkened, the artists' gorgeous blue banished. *Christ on His Way to the Praetorium* shows the might and power of the city against one man. *The Dark Crucifixion* is unbearable as an end, but for God the Father attentive in Heaven above. More than a book, a gift of shared emotion.

CHRISTMAS ONE YEAR brought me a silver tie clasp engraved with a Thai dancer brandishing an uplifted bow in his left hand. On the card, Mrs. Roosevelt wrote in her sometimes indecipherable handwriting: "Dear Will— Just a little remembrance I got for you in Bangkok, which I hope you can wear in _____ and _____. Best wishes and affectionate thoughts. —Eleanor R."

A touch of mystery is part of all intimate relationships!

ON THE DAY that President Tito of Yugoslavia was coming to Val-Kill Cottage for lunch, Mrs. Roosevelt organized her house guests, including my mother and myself, into a four-car caravan and we headed for the Roosevelt gravesite to meet her distinguished guest, who was to place a wreath on the grave of Franklin D. Roosevelt.

A mile or so from our destination we made a stop at a cabinetmaker's shop. We knew it was to be for just a few minutes, and that only my mother and myself would accompany Mrs. Roosevelt inside.

Once inside, Mrs. Roosevelt was as excited as a child on Christmas morning. She led us to a bench where the cabinetmaker was working. Having expected her, he jumped up and led us to inspect his craftsmanship.

"See," Mrs. Roosevelt showed us, "this is to be your Christmas present from me. I hope you will like it—a perfectly made copy of my grandmother Hall's mahogany gateleg coffee table. I know you've always admired it when we use it for after-dinner coffee by the fireplace. The top, when it's not opened for use, is only five inches wide. Won't that be wonderful to have in your home? I love mine!"

We murmured thanks and expressed admiration for the handsome hand finishing. Indeed, except for wear, one could not tell them apart.

When bidding Mrs. Roosevelt good night, I added, wonderingly, "I couldn't imagine what was so important this morning when we were excitedly on our way to meet President Tito. The procession of cars lined up outside the shop and your guests waiting . . . because you were so enthusiastic to show us our wonderful present still being created!"

Gently, she replied, "Why should that seem unusual, Bill? I may never see Mr. Tito again, but you are a friend and always will be."

MRS. ROOSEVELT HAD RETURNED from her month-long trip to the Soviet Union in 1957 full of wondrous stories. I was particularly eager to hear about her trips to Tashkent and Samarkand in Central Asia.

The two-thousand-mile jet flight from Moscow took four hours. Mrs. Roosevelt told me that, landing in Tashkent, she was surprised to see they were surrounded by a vast desert. "Suddenly, before we drove into the city, we saw a towering cloud of sand out in the desert moving rapidly in our direction. It seems I was to be welcomed by an important chieftain who, in the midst of Russian conformity, lived untamed in a desert vastness with his people. When the horsemen became visible, we were impressed with their huge horses and intrepid, skillful riding. Reaching our party, a courier of a sort was sent to escort me into the presence of the chief. I was later told it was an unprecedented honor. No one seemed to know how he found out that I was arriving, nor, for that matter, how he knew who I was—anything not 'arranged' by the Communists perplexed them in a most unpleasant way. By the time I walked the short distance toward the assembled troop of horsemen, a large tent had been erected as if by magic, and the sand at its entrance and interior covered with magnificent rugs, largely red in color. It was like an episode out of *Arabian Nights*. I was greeted by the great man with a powerful masculine graciousness, as if to be in each other's presence was the most wonderful thing in the world. We shared a delicious drink, unidentifiable to me, but sweet without being cloying. I was then ceremoniously presented with this miniature sword."

The object was seven inches long, primitively made, the brass beaten and fitted with a hard wood handle that was bound in brass. Cut into the blade was XANIA-KPHTH. The brass sheath ended in a small head, so stylized that it might represent a bird or beast. The entire surface of the sheath was covered with grain and flower motifs. Hanging from two two-inch chains of tiny links were two symbols: a small round medallion with a geometric design and a thin indefinable symbol cut out in sharp detail almost like a word in a language unknown to us. Perhaps a gilt wash accounts for the brightness to which it polishes. It seemed that none of Mrs. Roosevelt's guides had ever seen its likes. Someone opined that it was a painstaking copy of a historic ceremonial treasure.

"Whatever it is," Mrs. Roosevelt told me, "it was presented to me as the highest honor possible. I want you to have it, William. I give everything to the library, but this they will have to do without. It is special and I love its mystery and the gloriously dramatic way it came to me. It will be perfect on your desk."

⊰⊱

Mrs. Roosevelt loved to open doors for William Turner Levy. On one occasion, he was invited to lecture on T. S. Eliot at West Point by General William Westmoreland, whose guest he was at a formal dinner at the commandant's headquarters.

⊰⊱

ONE EVENING, in a conversation with Mrs. Roosevelt, I criticized a visitor she had entertained that afternoon for what I considered a rude question he had asked.

She looked at me gently and, putting her hand lightly on my arm, said, "You must be understanding and accept people as they are."

I'm glad I remembered her words because at the time I didn't realize how much I was being told.

I LEARNED ANOTHER important lesson on one of the innumerable Sunday nights when Mrs. Roosevelt and I were driving back to town after a weekend at Hyde Park. I suddenly realized that I had passed the parkway exit for her house. Perhaps I was engrossed in our conversation. Perhaps, after she handed me a dime for the toll on the Henry Hudson Bridge, I was still musing on the fact that only she could present a coin with the noble incus, or portrait, of her husband on it.

"Gosh," I said, lamely, "I passed the exit." It was clear that the solution was to get off at the next exit and backtrack on the local streets.

Once at the house, our usual routine enforced itself. Mrs. Roosevelt sat at her desk to read and sign her mail and I looked around and found something to read. New books and worldwide periodicals were constantly appearing.

Halfway through her hour-long chore, she took time off to explore the kitchen and she called to me, "There's some apple pie here, just waiting for us!"

We carried sizable portions and glasses of milk to our respective seats. The pools of light from the lamps made the approach to midnight cozy.

Knowing that Mrs. Roosevelt had an early flight to Buffalo in the morning, I apologized as we bade each other farewell. "We lost a good twenty-five minutes by my missing the exit. I'm really sorry, especially as you have to get up so early."

She smiled and said, "Well, William, just don't do it again."

A temperate reply: not making too much of my false step, but not dismissing it either. A temperate reply.

For many years now, I have been gifted with a rare resource. Whenever I am faced with a true complexity, I ask myself, "What would Mrs. Roosevelt have done?" I have always been blessed with the answer. More than once it has been difficult to fulfill.

჻

Mrs. Roosevelt on occasion turned to William Turner Levy for counsel. As she was no ordinary woman, she faced extraordinary perplexities; for example, what gift to send to a queen!

჻

Sometimes I was the one giving guidance. There was an infinite variety to Mrs. Roosevelt's contacts. Anticipation was useless, so one was always in happy expectation!

"I'm baffled, William," Mrs. Roosevelt said to me, "I can't think of what to send Queen Elizabeth and the family this Christmas. Do you have any suggestions?"

This was not a question I had been asked before. I said, "It must be American and it should be simple."

After a moment's reflection, I was inspired. "How about Vermont maple syrup?"

Mrs. Roosevelt acquiesced at once, "Perfect!"

Some weeks later I was privileged to read the warmly appreciative thank you message on Buckingham Palace stationery.

MRS. ROOSEVELT SHOWED ME a letter from a boy in the South who, wanting to augment his mother and father's meager income by taking a newspaper route, asked for a twenty-five-dollar loan to buy a bicycle.

She had passed the letter to me over my left shoulder as I was seated on a sofa, reading with my back to her desk so as not to distract her from her nightly ritual of dealing with her correspondence. She would make notes for an appropriate reply on the letter that her secretary would type up the next day. A second pile of letters on her desk were the ones readied for her signature from the previous day's mail. Two hundred letters a day was average, but after she made a public statement or participated in a newsworthy event it would rise to the thousands.

"What do you think?" she asked, referring to the letter she had given me.

I replied that it appeared perfectly genuine, but how can one be sure?

"You're right. I'll make sure. I'll write to the Episcopal clergyman in that town and ask him to check it out."

Not long after, Mrs. Roosevelt beamingly reported to me, "That boy has his bicycle!"

❧

There were also times when each of the two friends could rescue the other from awkward situations. She tried to spare him the embarrassment of hearing an unkind assessment of his flower arrangement skills, while he spared her an unwanted ride home with a Rotary Club officer after her talk to his organization.

❦

ON ONE OF MY week-long stays at Val-Kill Cottage, I became aware that Mrs. Roosevelt had an early-morning outside appointment and did not have time to cut and arrange flowers on a day when I knew guests were coming to lunch.

Copying her approach, I took a basket out to the flower garden, cut suitable blooms and, upon returning to the house, placed them in strategic vases and put together a blue-and-yellow centerpiece.

I must admit that I was pleased with the result and anticipated Mrs. Roosevelt's appreciation. It was something I had been able to do for her.

Mrs. Roosevelt greeted me upon her return and I rather proudly pointed out my achievement. She thanked me, and I went upstairs to write a letter.

Later, descending the stairs to put my letter with the outgoing mail, I heard a voice from around the corner.

Mrs. Roosevelt's niece was saying, "*Who* arranged the flowers? They're *dreadful!*"

Mrs. Roosevelt replied, "Not so loud. He may hear you. William did it. Don't let him hear you, and don't say anything to him. After all, perhaps just a little shift here and there and they'll be quite presentable. They're bright and fresh and the *centerpiece* is quite attractive."

Mrs. Roosevelt was determined to save my face.

IT PLEASED ME WHEN I could be the one to ease the situation for Mrs. Roosevelt. One evening, because I expressed a desire to hear her deliver a lecture, Mrs. Roosevelt invited her daughter-in-law Anne, Maureen Corr, and me to accompany her to a Rotary Club dinner in a prosperous upstate New York town. Mrs. Roosevelt told me that a particular procedure was more or less the norm on these occasions. She was invited to speak on the United Nations, which is why she accepted—especially as the community was solidly Republican, then one member of the committee would pick her up and have the privilege of driving her to the town. At either his home or that of another member of the committee, she would have cocktails or pause to freshen up. Another member of the committee would drive her to the dinner, and in some cases, another to the auditorium in which she was to speak, and yet another would drive her home.

"The *difficulty* is," she told me, "that I have to speak, give miniature talks, and some not so miniature, to each of these individuals—which makes for a fairly exhausting evening. It is made to appear as a compliment, but it is actually very inconsiderate, though no doubt unintentionally so. If Tubby were to drive me, I could read or nap en route."

I told her I thought it was a dreadful imposition.

"Well, tonight you may put your foot down and *insist* that I come home in our car. I have promised to allow the designated member of the Rotary Club to drive me up."

Anne Roosevelt drove Maureen Corr and me. We trailed the slow-moving car carrying Mrs. Roosevelt and noted through its rear window that Mrs. Roosevelt was indeed talking most of the hour-long trip. We arrived at the Rotarian's home and were greeted by his wife, who ushered us in. Would we like sherry or tomato juice? Anne and I looked so unhappy—intentionally—that the gentleman half-whispered the suggestion that we might have a martini or a whiskey. Anne and I chose martinis, Maureen a whiskey on the rocks, after Mrs. Roosevelt had accepted the sherry. Our host and hostess then reversed their stance and drank whiskey. The drinks were served in very small glasses, but I managed to get the three of us a refill.

We spent some twenty-five minutes making idle conversation before the doorbell rang and another committeeman appeared to drive Mrs. Roosevelt to the local school where the dinner was to be held and her speech given. We had had time before that, however, to see the house's chief attraction, a plush television room, of great interest to all of us who had never seen one before. The chairs were luxuriously comfortable and all faced the television set. Drapes, we were shown, could be drawn to shut out the sunlight for daytime viewing. I excused myself to use the bathroom. There I found an interior decorator's wildest ideas given free rein.

The hostess's costume jewelry was framed in many velvet-lined shadow boxes to serve as pictures decorating the walls. Anne Roosevelt, who viewed the exhibition at my suggestion, emerged with less than a straight face.

As we were about to leave, our hostess proffered a box of Sen-Sen, a breath sweetener! Mrs. Roosevelt did not act surprised, but I thought Anne Roosevelt would die of stupefaction. Timidly, it was explained by our host and hostess, who partook of the pellets, that some of the members of the club didn't approve of drinking, and that they did have to live with them. I was bold enough to say, taking the liberty of speaking for our party, that we didn't really care what other persons thought about something once we had chosen to do it.

At the school, without asking if she'd like them or if they might damage her dress, a corsage of eight roses was pinned on Mrs. Roosevelt. Anne Roosevelt bridled just a bit as a corsage of *six* roses was pinned onto her dress. Maureen Corr very pleasantly accepted her status symbol of a *four*-rose corsage. I couldn't imagine what would have been my fated number had I been a lady!

Dinner, the usual unimaginative creamed chicken and peas, began with a glass of apricot nectar. I avoided catching Anne Roosevelt's eyes as she sipped the unfamiliar liquid with obvious distaste. The woman on my right must have been important locally, for she had a six-carnation corsage. She informed me most open-mindedly (she thought) that although she heartily disapproved of Mrs. Roosevelt politically, she felt that they should all hear both sides on the UN. I refrained from replying, but wondered what other side there could possibly be.

Mrs. Roosevelt's speech was a triumph. I had wondered how she would probe to find a line of sympathetic communication with the audience. Her opening sentence was, "Do you know how much the United Nations costs each and every one of us a year?" Since the answer was in cents, it proved a superb opening remark to make to this conservative audience. The rest of her enthralling speech, peppered with wonderful anecdotes, proved to her audience what a bargain they were getting for their money. I was convinced that she made many friends for the UN that night.

I did have to rescue Mrs. Roosevelt from a ride back to Hyde Park with the club officer honored with that role. He was reasonable enough when I explained the circumstances, but he asked to be allowed to drive Mrs. Roosevelt a few blocks or so out of town (she could then transfer to our car), so as not to be humiliated in the eyes of his friends. It was so arranged. I thought of the force of Yeats's remark that he admired the aristocrats who were above fear, and the poor who were beneath it, but had no use for those in the middle.

Before retiring that night, Mrs. Roosevelt and I had bananas and glasses of milk in a corner of the dark living room encircled in overlapping pools of light from two lamps. I was hoping that she didn't consider my observations about the evening's activities too unkind, for they weren't intended to be.

"The trouble is," she said sadly, "that these people know so little and they think they know so much." She asked if I thought she did well, and I expressed my admiration for a perfect performance, admitting that I wouldn't have known what to say.

"You have to know people—it's a matter of experience. My husband really knew people, this kind of people, all kinds—down to the ground. As a boy he grew up on a country estate with servants of all classes, from grooms to the butler. He went riding with his father as soon as he was able to mount a horse and would greet friends and neighbors, tradesmen, relations, so he was totally at ease with all sorts and conditions of men. And he *enjoyed* what there was to enjoy in each contact."

Mrs. Roosevelt looked at me with a glint of amusement in her eyes. "William, did you notice one thing in particular in the house where we stopped first?"

I said no, nothing beyond what I had already mentioned.

"There wasn't a single book in the house," she exclaimed, "and didn't that look strange!"

I was forced to correct her. There were four, I told her, in a small table next to the chair I had sat in: *Selections from the Bible, A Book of Etiquette, Selections from the Reader's Digest*, and *A Book of Famous Quotations*.

⚬⚬⚬

One of the bonds that drew William Turner Levy and Eleanor Roosevelt together was their shared faith.

⚬⚬⚬

SITTING QUIETLY TOGETHER after tea one autumn after-noon at Hyde Park, we fell into expressions of our delight in each other's company, and in the course of our conver-sation, we found ourselves speaking of our faith.

I volunteered that although I was born into the protec-tion of the church and had been a devout boy and young man both inwardly and in outer attendance and practice, it was the war experience that confirmed my faith. Not the evil of our enemies, so much as my daily shared life with the men in the Army. I found in both camp life and in the test of the front line itself that men were both better and worse than I had imagined.

In a common uniform, stripped of all social pressure, I saw evil (things done to others' harm) and good (sublimely unself-conscious sacrifice) beyond my conception. For the first time I fully believed in Heaven and Hell.

Mrs. Roosevelt, thoughtful for a while, placed her hand on my knee, looked at me with her eyebrows raised above her searching eyes, and said, "If there is no God, all things are permissible," adding that she remembered that from *The Brothers Karamazov*.

It was on this occasion that I shared with her a prayer that I used daily: "Help me, Lord God, in my good pur-pose and in thy service and grant me this day to begin perfectly; for naught it is that I have done unto this time." I had found it in *The Imitation of Christ* by Thomas à Kempis, in a 1943 edition, roughly five hundred years after it was written, edited by my former teacher and friend Irwin Edman, a professor of philosophy at Columbia University. Indeed, I carried the book with me all my years in the Army and have it still. At her request later that day, I wrote it out for her. She was to tell me a few years later that she always used it upon arising.

Also, several years later, she told me that she was going the very next day to be speaking to the inmates of a women's prison located in Greenwich Village, New York.

She confessed, "I'm terrified. What can I say to them that would mean anything? The fact of the matter is, I walk in, I'm with them, but then *I* walk out, free. I don't know how I got myself into such a situation. Oh, yes, I do. The date was many months off when I accepted it—and I did so thoughtlessly."

I was stunned by the realistic appraisal of her situation. I telephoned her the next evening.

She told me, "I smiled in that great cage of a room. I was terrified. Then I knew what I had to do. As I was being introduced, I said the Lord's Prayer, asked our Father's help, and then stood up on the podium."

There was a moment of silence on the line. I asked, "How did it go?"

Meekly, she answered me, "It was wonderful. Such applause. Such tears." After a brief pause, she said, "Our faith—it is what enables us."

When I sat next to her in Saint James's Church, Hyde Park, in the Roosevelt pew (the only one not reupholstered, in deference, I assume, to the President's memory), and we received the sacrament of the Holy Communion (this happened on just one occasion, for the church was "low" in its Episcopal leanings and the sacrament was celebrated only once a month), I could not but sense her complete separation from all earthly ties, caught up in a loving absorption. I had experienced this "absence" of another only once before, when kneeling beside T. S. Eliot at the Church of Saint Mary the Virgin in New York—the worshipping self caught up in rapture, almost a physical levitation.

THE GREAT TEACHER in Mrs. Roosevelt's life was the French mistress Mlle. Souvestre at the British girls' school Mrs. Roosevelt attended. This remarkable woman was the first person in her life to help her gain confidence by having confidence in her. Mlle. Souvestre entrusted her with responsibilities, such as purchasing tickets for student trips, and having confidence reposed in her gave the shy young woman the experience that strengthened her sense of her own value. All her life, Mrs. Roosevelt liked to acknowledge that debt. It pained her, however, to recall that her fine mentor was devoid of religious faith.

One late evening in 1960, Mrs. Roosevelt shared with me her final thoughts about this. "You know, Bill, Mlle. Souvestre claimed she was an atheist. Not to all, or at first, but I traveled a good deal with her. I learned that she was most impatient with persons who, as she would say, needed rewards to be good. She felt, very simply and very firmly, that you did the right thing for its own sake. And you did it because you knew it was the *right* thing, the only thinkable thing to do. But now that I think about it, it seems no one could possibly trust his or her opinion of what was right—

and neither did she. She simply refused—and I suppose it was pride—to acknowledge that she was following standards she hadn't invented. She was following love, as we all must, and that is to follow God."

LATE ONE NIGHT Mrs. Roosevelt and I were discussing Alain Resnais' film, *Hiroshima, Mon Amour*. With a strangely distant look in her eyes, she intoned the word "Hiroshima," and said, "They brought it upon themselves. It was like a Biblical destruction. What evil there is in the heart of man! Were it conceived by a writer or a painter, it would be a depraved scene, utterly destructive, anti-human—yet our eyes looked upon a reality."

MRS. ROOSEVELT KNEW that in the spring of 1957 I had delivered a lecture entitled "The Idea of the Church in T. S. Eliot" at the Cathedral of Saint John the Divine in New York. The research and the writing were scrupulous, for what could be a more exacting task than writing of a man's religious beliefs?

I gave permission for it to be published in *The Christian Scholar*, several copies of which, printed in individual format, I sent to Eliot. Tom wrote, "Prior to your work, all I received was abusive criticism. There was no attempt to understand and define my position. I cannot tell you how grateful I am that this is now available." Later, in person, he urged me to develop it into a longer study, promising to provide any assistance I might require.

After reading her copy several times, Mrs. Roosevelt spoke of its personal value to her, "Isn't it a splendid exposition of our common faith?" Pausing, she added, "Mr. Eliot's ability to share his profound commitment has helped me to clarify and shape my own." Next, she said, "I am so happy you've undertaken to do a similar service for Franklin."

THE TELEPHONE RANG at 7 A.M. At that hour, I knew who it was.

"Good morning! This is Eleanor Roosevelt, William."

I spoofed British telephone lingo. "Oh, are you there? Did you ring up?"

Easily amused, Mrs. Roosevelt rejoined, "I'm traipsing off to Columbus in a few minutes. Just was curious what you're up to in your American literature class this morning."

"Still in *Moby-Dick*," I said, "and today it's that fabulous chapter on 'The Whiteness of the Whale.' Melville concludes that we all need spectacles to look at the world and make sense of it. He says, otherwise, we're like willful travelers in Lapland refusing to wear sunglasses and, therefore, like the wretched infidel who gazes himself blind staring at the whiteness. It is sure to lead to a grand discussion of the relative value of this pair of glasses or that. Who knows, surely someone will come up with seeing the world through the perspective of faith?"

"I wish I could be there, tucked invisibly in the corner," Mrs. Roosevelt said.

The art of friendship: to give one's friend a sense of the value of what he's doing; to enlarge that classroom and place its lesson on a plane flying west.

Chapter 13

Saying Good-bye

THE DAY CAME WHEN Father William Turner Levy was called on to give a final gift to his dear friend—that of presiding at her funeral and burial services. Eleanor Roosevelt, First Lady of the World, died on November 7, 1962, and was laid to rest in the Rose Garden at Hyde Park, next to her husband, Franklin Delano Roosevelt.

She had left, said Adlai E. Stevenson in his eulogy, "a name to shine on the entablatures of truth. Forever." And so it did, and does. But for William Turner Levy, as for other devoted friends, Mrs. Roosevelt's name would shine forever in a different place—the deepest recesses of the heart.

⸻

BIRTH, OVER WHICH we have no control, is when we begin to die. Life lived according to His will is for us to choose. And death? In our end is our beginning.

Not everyone is privileged to know when he will die. Not everyone would choose to know. Mrs. Roosevelt did know. I cannot say if that would have been her choice. I do know what she did with the knowledge.

One evening at Val-Kill when we two night owls were alone as usual, Mrs. Roosevelt confided, "Dr. Gurewitsch has told me that I have two years to live. It's a blood problem that involves the bone marrow. This," she showed me a small amber-colored jar, "is the medicine that I will be taking. It will work beautifully—but only for two years."

I must have frowned, for she flashed a reassuring smile, saying, "Well, that's more than many people can count on. The important thing is that I use the time well. Less important things must just go by the board. So, William, from now on we must have three dates on our calendars at all times! Three's the great number, you know!"

Rising, she went to her desk, produced her appointment book, and urged, "Now, run upstairs, get your book, and we'll get started right away!"

Her almost conspiratorial mood, with its promise of good times ahead, worked her intended magic. Almost lightheartedly, I all but dashed upstairs. In the two minutes it took me to return to her, she had produced a chilled bottle of Moët & Chandon—brut 1947—and two glasses.

ANNA ROOSEVELT HALSTED telephoned me on November 7. "Bill, Mother slipped away almost two hours ago. The family wanted you to know before we announce it publicly. Will you take the services, both at the church and at the gravesite? For as you know, that was Mother's wish. We know you will be tactful in regard to Mr. Kidd. He *is* the rector of Saint James's and a dear man. Please find enough for him to do in the service and we'll ask him to do a short eulogy. We don't want him to be unhappy. Once again, you will be doing something very important for the family. And, Bill, our deepest sympathy to you."

Two hundred people were invited by telegram to the church service and one thousand to the gravesite in the Rose Garden where her husband was buried. They would be together now: she, who had made his life possible by preventing his doting mother from turning him into the invalid squire of Hyde Park after his polio attack in 1921 left him incapable of walking unaided, and he, who had risen to master leadership of the free world, liberated it, and made her life as the First Lady of the World possible.

Mrs. Roosevelt expressed to me her wish to have a private funeral immediately after her death and then the announcement that it was over. I had to tell her that she was being unrealistic. She agreed, then sighed. "Then, Will, a plain oaken casket with pine boughs cut from the estate on top. No flowers." That wish was honored.

The family did not invite the Bishop of New York, Horace W. B. Donegan, to participate in the services, but he invited himself by appearing. I saw to it that he had a suitable part in the church service and invited him to offer the final blessing at the gravesite. In keeping with Mrs. Roosevelt's request, however, I was last in the clergy procession as priest in charge.

The family was upset that President Kennedy was coming. They feared his presence would detract from the service itself. Their fears proved unwarranted: President and Mrs. Kennedy knew how to render themselves all but invisible. Both looked straight ahead, wholly intent upon the reason they had come. Following the casket out of the church, I glanced at the president standing at his seat on the aisle. His eyes caught mine and, in comradely recognition and undoubted sympathy, blinked a silent message.

Before the service, I had a few moments alone in the familiar, tiny church. I kneeled and prayed beside the casket. As I rose and took a white chrysanthemum from an altar vase for my prayer book, words from her letters formed in my mind, "I love to be with you. . . . I thought we all had fun! . . . My love and a thousand thanks for your constant thought and affection. . . . I am deeply grateful for your prayers."

Looking up at the congregation as the service began, I was incredulous. It was like a historic mosaic, a tribute of sorrowing faces: the family, children and grandchildren, backed by the President and the First Lady, the Trumans, Vice President Johnson, former President Eisenhower, Governor Rockefeller, Mayor Wagner, Adlai E. Stevenson, the Chief Justice, senators and congressmen, Herbert H. Lehman, Frances Perkins, James A. Farley, Anna Rosenberg, Francis Biddle—so many from the Roosevelt years.

There was a vast throng outside and at the gravesite. I was not being observant at that point, but I did notice Marian Anderson, one of many acknowledging a debt at a funeral where there were representatives, some in exotic dress, from nations whose existence had never been dreamed of in Mrs. Roosevelt's youth, but who now mourned her as a friend.

I spoke the commendation at the grave: "Unto Almighty God we commend the soul of our sister departed, and we commit her body to the ground. Earth to earth, ashes to ashes, dust to dust; in the sure and certain hope of the Resurrection unto eternal life, through our Lord Jesus Christ; at whose coming in glorious majesty to judge the world, the earth and the sea shall give up their dead; and the corruptible bodies of those who sleep in Him shall

The procession to Eleanor Roosevelt's gravesite at Hyde Park. The family asked me (front right) to preside at the services. Those present included, from left, Franklin D. Roosevelt, Jr., First Lady Jacqueline Kennedy, President John F. Kennedy, Vice President Lyndon B. Johnson, Harry S Truman, Bess Truman, Dwight D. Eisenhower, and Margaret Truman. This photograph appeared on the front pages of newspapers worldwide. *(Copyright © 1962 by* The New York Times. *Reprinted by permission.)*

be changed, and made like unto His own glorious body; according to the mighty working whereby He is able to subdue all things unto Himself."

Bishop Donegan invoked God's blessing upon us all. The plaintive strain of taps floated over our bowed heads and a gentle rain began to fall.

At the order of the president, all United States flags throughout the world were lowered to half-staff, the first time a president's widow was so honored.

Adlai E. Stevenson's words spoken in the General Assembly of the United Nations remain an imperishable tribute: "She would rather light candles than curse the darkness and her glow has warmed the world."

A MEMORIAL SERVICE in memory of Anna Eleanor Roosevelt (1884–1962) was held on November 17 in New York at the Cathedral Church of Saint John the Divine. Ten thousand persons filled the magnificent cathedral to overflowing.

The impressive processions that began and ended the service, the soaring music and song, the Bishop of New York's conduct of the service and the pulse-stirring rendition of our national anthem were the rituals of honor and affection by which we celebrate the life triumphant.

A commemorative prayer with choral response and the final blessing were delivered by the Right Reverend Arthur Lichtenberger, the presiding bishop of the Episcopal Church in the United States. I was named honorary chaplain to the presiding bishop and carried his pastoral staff before him at the end of the processions.

His Excellency Mr. Adlai E. Stevenson, permanent representative of the United States of America to the United Nations, spoke the eulogy.

He spoke with an eloquence that he alone possessed at that time in the English-speaking world.

"How much she had done—how much still unchronicled! We dare not try to tabulate the lives she salvaged, the battles—known and unrecorded—she fought, the afflicted she comforted, the hovels she brightened, the faces and places, near and far, that were given some new radiance, some sound of music, by her endeavors. What other single human being has touched and transformed the existence of so many others? What better measure is there of the impact of anyone's life?

"She imparted to the familiar language—nay, what too many have come to treat as the clichés—of Christianity a new poignancy and vibrance. She did so not by reciting them, but by proving that it is possible to live them. It is this above all that rendered her unique in her century. It was said of her contemptuously at times that she was a do-gooder, a charge levelled with similar derision against another public figure one thousand, nine hundred and sixty-two years ago.

"What we have lost in Eleanor Roosevelt is not her life. She lived that out to the full. What we have lost, what we wish to recall for ourselves, to remember, is what she was herself. And who can name it? But she left 'a name to shine on the entablatures of truth. Forever.'"

Index

Page references in italics indicate photographs.

251

About the Authors

William Turner Levy was born in New York City in 1922 and received his bachelor's degree from the City College of New York. He was awarded his M.A. and Ph.D. by Columbia University. During World War II, Dr. Levy won the Bronze Star medal for a reconnaissance mission to the Rhine. After the war, he was ordained a priest of the Episcopal Church. Dr. Levy retired as associate professor of English at the City University of New York in 1976. Since 1978, he has taught at Viewpoint School in Calabasas, California, and is currently its provost. He is coauthor with Victor Scherle of two books, *Affectionately, T. S. Eliot, the Story of a Friendship: 1947–1965*, and *The Films of Frank Capra*, reissued as *The Complete Films of Frank Capra*.

Cynthia Russett received her Ph.D. in history from Yale, where she is now professor of history. She teaches courses in modern American history with a special emphasis on cultural and intellectual history and the history of American women. Her most recent books are *Sexual Science: The Victorian Construction of Womanhood* and *Second to None: A Documentary History of American Women* (with Ruth Moynihan and Laurie Crumpacker).